D1263505

HOOK SPIN BUZZ

HOW TO COMMAND ATTENTION, CHANGE MINDS & INFLUENCE PEOPLE

GARRETT SODEN

PETERSON'S/PACESETTER BOOKS

PRINCETON, NEW JERSEY

Copyright © 1996 by Garrett Soden

All rights reserved. No part of this book may be reproduced, stored in a retrieval system, or transmitted, in any form or by any means—electronic, mechanical, photocopying, recording, or otherwise—except for citations of data for scholarly or reference purposes with full acknowledgment of title, edition, and publisher and written notification to Peterson's Guides prior to such use.

Hook Spin Buzz is published by Peterson's/Pacesetter Books.

Pacesetter Books, Peterson's/Pacesetter Books, and the Pacesetter horse design are trademarks of Peterson's Guides, Inc.

Library of Congress Cataloging-in-Publication Data

Soden, Garrett.
    Hook, spin, buzz : how to command attention, change minds, and influence people / Garrett Soden.
       p.   cm.
    Includes index.
    ISBN 1-56079-524-7
    1. Business communication. I. Title.
    HF5718.S636   1995
    650'.014—dc20   95-19052
                                              CIP

Creative direction by Linda Huber
Cover design by Susan Newman
Interior design by Cynthia Boone

Printed in the United States of America

10 9 8 7 6 5 4 3 2 1

Visit Peterson's Education & Career Center on the Internet (World Wide Web) at http://www.petersons.com

CONTENTS

Part ▯▯▯
Buzz: A Good Word

This book is dedicated to Scott David Ray.
Thanks for standing with me on broken road stones.

Human communication is not just a transfer of information like two fax machines connected with a wire; it is a series of alternating displays of behavior by sensitive, scheming, second-guessing, social animals. When we put words into people's ears we are impinging on them and revealing our own intentions, honorable or not, just as surely as if we were touching them.

—*Steven Pinker*, director of the Center for Cognitive Neuroscience, MIT, from his book *The Language Instinct*

By the right use of these things, a person may do the greatest good, and by the unjust use, the greatest mischief.

—*Aristotle* on rhetoric

ACKNOWLEDGMENTS

This book is the result of ideas I've had rumbling around in my head for several years. Although its concepts are drawn from more than two decades of communication experience as well as my lifelong interest in and study of persuasion, social psychology, politics, public relations, advertising, language, and visual design, it shouldn't be assumed that the authors from whom I've borrowed ideas are in any way responsible for how I've put those ideas to work here. The applications are my own, and any lapses in interpretation or understanding are also mine.

I'm most grateful to the people at Peterson's/Pacesetter for believing with me that a different kind of business communication book is needed. First and foremost my thanks go to my editor, Andrea Pedolsky, who has offered great support for and patience with the birth of this book, and to Jim Gish, whom I think of as a true visionary (as well as a damn good guitar player). I am also grateful to Bernadette Boylan, Lenore Greenberg, Laurie Schlesinger, Pam Wilkison, Linda Huber, Susan Newman, and Cynthia Boone, all of whom deserve kudos for their consistently professional work for Peterson's.

I also owe a debt of gratitude to the people who were kind enough to be interviewed: Betsy Amster, Jan Baird, Pat Bowie, Tom Harrison, Jack Montgomery, Kit Rachlis, and Scott Ray.

Thanks, too, to my daughter, Jordan Seider, who has endured long days of a secluded, writing father, and to Tom the Cat, who cares what I do, but not much.

Finally, I wish to give my deepest thanks, as always, to my wife, Denise K. Seider, who has contributed absolutely essential suggestions and constructive criticism to this book and who has also been a wellspring of love and support.

HOW THIS BOOK WILL IMPROVE YOUR COMMUNICATION

This book is about communication: business communication in particular and, specifically, *persuasive* business communication. I wrote it for two reasons.

First, like everyone else, I've noticed that the surge in new communication tools—from voice mail to e-mail to fax machines to cellular phones—means we spend more time than ever struggling with a tidal wave of incoming messages. It's difficult enough trying to sort through them all when you're on the receiving end, but when you're trying to reach someone with a vital message, it's frightening to think your best ideas might sink in the flood. It hardly matters how miraculous our forms of communication are if our messages can't catch and hold someone's attention, persuade them, and motivate them to take action.

It's a problem business communication specialists have mostly ignored. People in other fields, though, have made it their business to learn how to craft messages that not only float to the surface but seem to surf effortlessly into our consciousness. Social psychologists have collected sixty years' worth of research that pinpoints why people pay attention to one message and ignore another. Journalists, media professionals, advertisers, politicians, and others have developed techniques to make sure we get their messages and believe what they say. I know this because for the past twenty years, in the various stages of my career as a writer, editor, graphic designer, public relations manager, and director of corporate communication, I've studied the research and used the techniques myself.

I've used them to produce mass communication, such as publications, advertising, and public relations campaigns, and I've used scaled down versions in my personal communication. I thought that if I could adapt these ideas and techniques to everyday business communication, others could too, and that they might help people get their messages through the information overload.

That, current books about business communication seemed to me to miss the complexity of human interchange is the second reason why I wrote this book. Crack open a standard textbook and you're likely to find communication described as a "signal" transmitted by a "sender" through a "channel" to be picked up by a "receiver." Since no one I knew acted much like a machine when they had a meeting, read a memo, or made a phone call, I reasoned that this was a poor model on which to base advice about communication. The more I read variations of this theory, the more convinced I became that something new was needed.

The result is *Hook Spin Buzz*. The name is drawn from popular terms that describe how attention-getting, persuasive communication works. Good communicators first get us hooked with an appealing idea; they spin a story so that we come to see their point of view and maybe change our mind or accept their idea; and finally, because they know the dynamics of group communication, they manage their communication so that it starts a buzz, a stimulating tingle of interest we want to share.

What I've hoped to do here is to put the principles of persuasion as discovered by research psychologists together with the methods of professional communicators and to present them in a format you can use to make your personal business communication more effective.

The Psychology Behind Hook Spin Buzz

Because business is supposed to be rational, most business communicators haven't faced a simple fact: that people make many more decisions based on hunches, gut feelings, and intuition than they do on cool rationality. Psychological research has confirmed this, and neurological studies are beginning to show that the actual physical parts of the brain that handle emotion and intellect must both be engaged and working together to produce rationality. (In fact, if the seat of emotion in the brain is damaged—if someone's capacity for gut feelings is switched off—the result is a person who seems calm and in control but who will make one illogical decision after another.)

Hook Spin Buzz works because it appeals to gut feelings first and allows you to follow through with an appeal to the intellect afterward. This gut-feeling way of deciding has a name in psychology circles. It's called the *peripheral route* of decision-making (as opposed to the *central route*, which is a thorough examination of information). The bits of information we use to make decisions in the peripheral route also have a name: They're called *heuristics*.

A heuristic is any simple cue or habit of mind that we rely on as likely to help us make a good decision. One example of a heuristic is the influence of authority. That's the cue we take when we rely on the advice of an expert. We assume an expert knows the answer, so we might not bother to find out more. Another heuristic is *social proof*, which is the habit we have of believing that if most

3

people think a certain way, there must be something to it. It's the heuristic that might cause you to think a restaurant is good simply because it's so crowded you can't get in.

As you've probably already guessed, today's information overload forces us to use the peripheral route more often, searching messages for heuristics that will make our decisions easier. Social psychologist Robert B. Cialdini points this out:

> I have recently become impressed by evidence suggesting that the form and pace of modern life is not allowing us to make fully thoughtful decisions, even on many personally relevant topics. That is, sometimes the issues may be so complicated, the time so tight, the distractions so intrusive, the emotional arousal so strong, or the mental fatigue so deep that we are in no cognitive condition to operate mindfully. Important topic or not, we have to take the shortcut route.

But most business communicators have no idea how to build heuristics into their messages. How to create heuristics and add them to your messages is one of the communication techniques you'll learn from this book.

What Hook Spin Buzz Does

Hook Spin Buzz is a method you can use to add a heuristic road map to your messages so that someone can take the peripheral route and get to the core of your ideas quickly. That doesn't mean you can skimp on solid research, tight reasoning, and lucid thinking. Someone who's been guided to your ideas by heuristics should be rewarded with substance; otherwise they'll resent being tricked into making a wasted trip. "The whole point is to find that honest, identifiable, valid thing to emphasize," says Jack Montgomery, a technical marketing consultant in the chemical industry. "What you can't do is come up with something that doesn't bear scrutiny."

In this book I'll show you how heuristics work and how to use them. I'll introduce you to people in business who've turned heuristics into hooks, spins, and buzzes in their day-to-day communication. The three-part format of this book follows that of the Hook Spin Buzz process:

First, the Hook: Where you'll learn to create an appeal that gets your audience interested in what you have to say.

Next, the Spin: Where you'll discover how to guide your audience's perception in a way that makes them see your idea from your point of view.

And last, the Buzz: Where you'll find out how to infuse your communication with the qualities that cause people to act or word to spread.

Hook Spin Buzz works in any kind of business communication—oral, written, e-mailed, faxed, face-to-face—because it's based on how we absorb information, not on the form of the information. In a letter, for example, your first paragraph might present the hook, while the next several paragraphs present a single spin (or several spins) that support the hook. The last paragraph or sentence might work to create a buzz, whether just in the recipient's mind or in the world at large. You'd follow the same general form if you were giving a speech or writing an annual report.

But Hook Spin Buzz is more versatile than this description suggests, because every message doesn't have to use all three parts. You might leave a message on someone's voicemail that's all hook to motivate them to return your call. Or your audience might already be hooked. They've hired your company, let's say, and so you might move directly to spin to explain what's to be done.

Sometimes finding a hook might be difficult because your information is dry. In these cases, enough spin by itself can catch the attention of your audience. Other times, you'll find that although your idea isn't brand-new, it fits perfectly with an idea that's already buzzing through the company. Your hook, then, would link to that buzz, add spin, and recreate your idea as a new addition to mainstream thought.

Each of the book's three parts covers a phase in the Hook Spin Buzz process, while each chapter focuses on a single principle or technique of that phase. Reading the book straight through will give you an overview of how to craft messages using the different techniques. But I hope you'll also find the organization easy to refer to when you have an important message to send and you need to pick the right appeal.

HOOK:

An Instant Appeal

There's no black magic in a hook. It's not subliminal seduction, hypnotic suggestion, subconscious manipulation, carnival barking, or the hard sell. A hook is a very simple thing. A hook is that part of your message that gets your audience interested.

Although a hook is easy to understand, it's hard to create, for two reasons. First, you often won't know what information in your message will interest your audience. What may be a minor point to you may be the major reason they want to know more. If that point isn't emphasized at the beginning, you may lose your audience before you can make them aware of it.

The second difficulty is this: Many things that motivate people to pay attention to a message have little (and sometimes nothing) to do with the content. They may listen because they feel they owe you a favor or allegiance. They might consider you an expert or a gossip. They might pay attention to you because everyone else does. Or they might simply like you.

The first two chapters of this section offer techniques for answering the first question: What does your audience want? After that, each successive chapter focuses on the individual heuristics that can trigger attention.

The actual form of a hook will change depending on the length of your message, your audience, and the kind of communication you're engaged in.

In a memo, your hook should probably be completed by the second sentence; after that you can elaborate. In an annual report, the entire statement by the company CEO might be a hook. If you're making a point in a meeting, the first dozen words might be the hook. If you've got a plan to make the computer system more efficient, you might tell your boss you've got a money-saving idea, while you might tell the computer folks you've found a way to make their life easier. Same idea, different hooks.

Besides audience appeal, a hook has three other qualities: It must be short, easy to understand, and placed at the beginning of a message.

1

Know Your Audience

Because a hook is defined as something that interests your audience, the first task in creating one is to study your audience. In fact, the rule is fundamental to the entire Hook Spin Buzz process: Know your audience.

Most of us realize that it's not wise to shoot your mouth off without knowing the sensitivities of the person you're talking to and that it is easier to persuade someone if you know what's important to them. But Hook Spin Buzz goes further. Since the techniques used appeal to a person's emotions and intellect, it's important to get to know the whole person. And that means paying attention to things that might seem irrelevant to doing business.

Here's what Scott Ray, an audio company owner, does when he meets somebody:

I start by noticing everything I can. They wear a lot of jewelry, what does that tell me? I'm not sure. It tells me something, but I don't know what. They're nervous. They're jittery. What does that tell me? It could mean that they're highly energized, it could mean that they have a problem, it could mean they're a crook. It could mean they had too much coffee this morning.

Scott has no agenda in mind. He's not trying to decide the best way to craft a hook at this point. He's just listening and watching, applying the techniques of good observation:

Paying genuine attention. Paying attention is work. A good listener is someone who, when they miss something, isn't afraid to say, "I'm sorry, I got distracted. Can you say that again?" Most people fake their way through a lapse in concentration and play catch-up by tuning back in. They use context to figure out what they missed, pretending that nothing happened. This sloppy habit results in missing not only information but also the finer nuances, which are essential to crafting a hook.

Sending the right signals. Physical and verbal signals tell someone that you want to hear more or that you can't wait to talk about your ideas. You will learn more on the receptive side of the equation, especially if you don't fill all the dead air. A lingering silence will often nudge someone into revealing what they really think.

If you need to ask questions, don't load them. When Pat Bowie, a director of a social service agency, wants to find out what someone thinks, she speaks in generalities: "Talk to me. Where are things going? How are things going?" If she knows there's a problem, she acknowledges it but lets the other person define it. "I hear that there's some frustration," she'll say, which neither presumes what's frustrating or even who's frustrated.

In the kind of wrangling Pat gets involved in, communication is rapid, pulsing back and forth between several concerned parties. I asked Pat if she ever mentions who she's already talked to or what they said. Her answer was emphatic:

No. Never. I never use the name of somebody else. I just state it as, "Just fill me in. I'm not sure. I've been out of the loop. Let me know what's going on." So you just hear it directly from them. You haven't put in one iota of how you feel about anything or know about anything, even though you most often have already heard from one source or another.

This approach keeps her information pure. What keeps it flowing are small signs of encouragement: She keeps her eyes on the person talking, nods in agreement, says "Yeah," or "Uh-huh," or "I know what you mean," at appropriate times.

What will stop the flow is anything that's not in response to the conversation. Actions like jingling keys, or playing with a pencil, or looking out the window may seem innocent, but people will take these as cues to stop talking.

Listening for motives. Ask yourself why someone would say what they're saying. It may be candor, or they may be trying to influence your opinion. *How* they are trying to influence you can tell you what will influence *them*.

For example, people will often reveal what they really think by *denying* it. If a manager says, "I'm not a dictator, but I do set high goals for my people," it's likely that some people think he *is* a dictator, since it's the first issue he bothered to address. He might even admit this to himself—although he hopes to convince you otherwise. By divining the motive behind his words, you may uncover the psychic wound he's nursing and create a balm that will soothe it. In this case, a hook that would help him picture himself as a strict but fair leader would go a long way.

Listening across the gender line. Men and women communicate differently. Linguist Deborah Tannen puts it this way:

> Since women seek to build rapport, they are inclined to play down their expertise rather than display it. Since men value the position of center stage and the feeling of knowing more, they seek opportunities to gather and disseminate factual information.

No matter which sex you are, realize that when someone of the opposite sex is speaking, they are trying to tell you something. Men aren't "babbling" because they think they know everything and can never be wrong, and women aren't "whining" because the going got tough and they can't take it. They are trying to communicate.

If you are going to build an effective hook for someone of the opposite sex, you need to inhabit their world for a while. The universe of men and women at work is largely the same except for a portion that some people refer to as "girl talk" or "guy talk."

For example, you may be talking to Larry about the funding proposal, and Joe comes up and starts a conversation about football. This may not tell you about the proposal, but if you listen in you may learn a lot about Larry and Joe. Do they admire coolly calculated plays or risky brinkmanship? Do they praise maverick heroes or steadfast team players? The qualities they admire in sports are probably the same qualities they admire in business.

Suppose Debbie and Jan are talking about Jan's upcoming nuptials. How does she go about planning her wedding? Is it supremely organized or more free-flowing? Is she more concerned about who'll be insulted if not invited or about where she's going on her honeymoon?

All these are clues to an inner life that will help you know what these people value and what you can appeal to when you need to persuade them.

Clothing. Contrary to what most people think, what someone wears is less important than how much they care about it. Forget for the moment whether their taste runs to pinstripe suits or casual outfits. Do they seem to have carefully considered what they're wearing, or to have settled for something that is just adequate? That care indicates how much they value form over content; style over substance. People who devote no imagination to clothing generally distrust the surface of things. They are likely to believe "the proof is in the pudding" or "that's just window dressing." They may regard people who dress to impress as shallow.

Once you know that someone cares about what they wear, you can try to guess whether it indicates an aggressive or conservative attitude, although it's not likely to be accurate because clothing has become pure calculation. Disorganized managers strive to seem stable in Brooks Brothers button-downs, while timid bureaucrats try to exude élan in Armani suits.

Offices. To get a better sense of what's important to someone, look in their office. Life values are usually displayed prominently on the walls. Diplomas, certificates, or pictures of famous people (especially when the office dweller is posing with them) tell you that the person might respond well to a hook with the heuristic of authority in it. It also tells you that she's particular about authority—she may display her degree from Harvard because she feels it's superior to the run of the mill. If you're going to quote an expert's words to convince her, it better be an expert she respects.

An abundance of family photos or pictures of fishing buddies or volleyball teammates might mean the person is someone to whom ties of loyalty are paramount. His concern is who's backing whom. For him, a hook that emphasizes a heuristic based on social proof might appeal.

Dan, a friend of mine who is the director of communications at a nonprofit agency, has on his office wall framed copies of a newspaper column he wrote more than twenty years ago. He also has a poster featuring a cartoon of a hard-boiled journalist in shirtsleeves with a press pass stuck in the headband of his fedora. The cartoon reporter is shouting into a phone. "Hello, sweetheart," he snarls, "Get me rewrite!" The poster and framed columns reveal a truth about Dan: In spite of the succession of public relations jobs he's had, he still thinks like a reporter. He likes hard facts, is unimpressed with titles, and has the demeanor of a cynical city editor, which is what he once was. Hooks that might work on someone else—an authority's endorsement or a play to sympathy—won't get far with Dan.

Books, magazines, software boxes, the style of furniture (if it's their choice), whether the computer looks used or neglected, whether there are signs of a recent out-of-office experience (a gym bag for an after-hours workout or plane tickets for a business trip)—almost everything people put in their offices says something about them.

Key words. People have personal vocabularies filled with words or phrases that make up a magical lexicon and that advertise what's important to them. I once had a boss who liked to say "a win-win situation," as if that utterance had the power to make it so. She used the phrase to try to equalize what was really a lopsided situation: Our small, nonprofit agency depended entirely on the largess of a huge metropolitan transportation agency. The phrase helped her say, in effect, "Look, this isn't charity. We offer you something valuable for your money." I found she was motivated by hooks that increased her authority, because they helped balance the power between our company and our funder.

In most fields, some common words become freighted with extra meaning. "Family values" was once a simple idea, and now it's a political football. The same thing happens in business. Pat Bowie told me that in her world of social service agencies, the word "prevention" is volatile. The debate about what prevention is has become crucial because funding dollars are now flowing to agencies that offer "prevention programs." To Pat, the word "prevention" offers a potential hook although it is also a potential land mine.

Sometimes an audience will fail to respond to a hook not because the appeal is wrong but because the words that describe it are. "You all may be talking about the same thing," Pat says, "and not even recognize it because the words aren't the same across disciplines."

Preferred information modes. A good hook is one that employs the right appeal, but a great hook is one that delivers that appeal in the form that the audience prefers. Harvard psychologist Howard Gardner has reported that we have seven different kinds of intelligences—musical, linguistic, logical-mathematical, spatial, bodily kinesthetic, intrapersonal, and interpersonal—and that we respond best to information that speaks to our natural inclination.

It's one reason the statistician in research might not see eye-to-eye with the art director in advertising: Their information supply lines don't connect.

Clues to a person's information preference are often in their job title. It's a good bet that tax attorneys are logical–mathematical, and writers are linguistic. You can also guess that engineers are spatial, and the staff in personnel is gifted in interpersonal communication. There are other clues for the other types: The musically minded might have Mozart playing in her office; a bodily kinesthetic may peddle his bike to work and park it under ski posters; an intrapersonal might keep his own counsel and spend his lunches alone.

Beyond sending numbers to digitmeisters, words to the literati, and graphs to the spatially gifted, strategies for dealing with the rest of the spectrum are more subtle. Someone musical will be especially sensitive to pitch changes in your voice; a whine, a sigh, a monotone, or high and low voice modulations will give them extra information. A bodily kinesthetic will respond to physical demonstrations; interpersonals and intrapersonals relate to a message's emotional content: Is it exciting, scary, funny, pathetic, or boring?

Mood. You can guess that if Ron has a toothache, there are probably better times to ask him for a raise. The psychological principle at work here is called *association,* which simply means that when we experience two things together, we think of them as connected, whether there is a true connection or not. Association might cause Ron to think of your request as a pain—it has certainly caused stranger connections, as when TV weather reporters get hate mail from people who blame them for floods or droughts (believe it or not, this is true).

Whatever mood your audience is in when you try to communicate, that's the association they will have with your effort. No hook will work on a bad day, but a weak one might when someone is feeling successful and has already said yes a few times.

It's sometimes possible to influence the mood of your audience before you cast a hook. For example, the reason so many deals are sealed over lunch isn't just to squeeze more working hours into the day. Research has shown people often swallow more than their meal when they're eating. One experiment found that serving food increased the acceptance of political statements. And the effect was undetectable: Later, the subjects couldn't remember which ideas had arrived with the food, and which had not.

More often, you can't create circumstances that produce a positive mood, but you can avoid negative ones. Five minutes before the close of a meeting is not the time to introduce your grand plan—people want to leave, and your plan will be associated with aggravated impatience.

Observing, listening, and thinking about your audience will help you inhabit the mind of your audience and enable you to imagine what your message will look like to them. "The idea is to work yourself into a position so you can understand how they're going about it, what their thoughts are, how they're coming around to their ideas," says Scott Ray. "The more you do that, the more you start to get an intuition about what it is that may be appealing to them from their point of view."

2

Don't Sell Your Seed, Sell Their Lawn

It's often hard to keep in mind a simple truth about people: that no matter how open and helpful they seem, they are generally less interested in our ideas than in what our ideas can do for them. Knowing your audience only helps, then, if that knowledge lets you see your ideas from their point of view. Some people never seem to really understand this. They try, but sound like the character in the *New Yorker* cartoon who turned to his companion and said, "Well, enough about me. What do *you* think about me?"

It's an easy mistake to make. It happens because we focus so intently on what we think is important to shape an idea in the first place that we become too close to it to see it. After creating a report, you've got to turn around and imagine you're a reader who's never seen this report before. And further, you must imagine you don't care about the report's author: that is, you.

In politics, a truism coined by long-time Speaker of the House Tip O'Neill was this: All politics is local. By that he meant that people care about what affects them, not the "bigger issues." Congressman William J. Hughes of New Jersey found this out when he began a town meeting in Salem County by saying that he was their national representative and didn't deal with things like potholes and trash pickup. But when the questions started, one woman stood up and said, "Well, I want to tell you, they're supposed to pick up my trash on Thursday afternoons and they never do and the dogs get into it." The point is, you can't control what people want, even if you think you know better than they do what they need.

At the public relations agency where Senior Vice President Tom Harrison works, they have a saying that reminds them to keep this in mind: "Don't sell our seed; sell their lawn." By that they mean, "Don't focus on what we think is wonderful about our work; focus on what it will do for our clients." For example, Tom's agency produces television commercials for an international relief agency that solicits donations to help people in trouble. Their camera crews travel the world capturing vivid images of people going through wars, famine, and natural disasters. But when Tom talks to the client about a commercial, he doesn't say things like "Notice how beautifully the setting sun illuminates that child's face? Isn't that a wonderful use of natural light?" He points out qualities in the commercial that will get people to send donations.

When Kit Rachlis, a newspaper editor in Los Angeles, went to the paper's financial officer with a request for a larger budget to hire editors, he didn't talk about beautiful writing. He talked about the bottom line:

When I would write memos about reinvesting on the editorial side, I always put them in terms of why I thought they were good commercial decisions. It wasn't just that it was good for journalism, and it wasn't just the right ethical and moral decision. Because I didn't believe those two reasons, in this particular case, would be persuasive. I happen to think that those things are true and that those values shouldn't be dismissed, but that the strongest argument to be made to that particular man, who had fiduciary responsibility of the paper, was to say that this reinvestment would redound commercially on to the organization and that therefore it was a good business decision, not just a good journalistic decision.

Creating a hook is like creating an advertisement for your ideas, and the people in advertising know that it is vital to keep your audience's interest in mind. Long-time advertising executive John Caples put it this way:

I have seen one mail order advertisement actually sell not twice as much, not three times as much, but 19 ½ times as much goods as another. Both advertisements occupied the same space. Both were run in the same publication. Both had photographic illustrations. Both had carefully written copy. The difference was that one used the right appeal and the other used the wrong appeal.

Rosser Reeves, one of the most revered advertising writers of the past fifty years, realized in the 1940s that most ads fail because most copywriters ignore the audience and instead try to show off—a practice he abhorred:

I'm not saying that charming, witty and warm copy won't sell. I'm just saying that I've seen thousands of charming, witty campaigns that didn't. Let's say you are a manufacturer. Your advertising isn't working and your sales are going down. And everything depends on it. Your future depends on it, your family's future depends on it, other people's families depend on it. And you walk in this office and talk to me, and you sit in that chair. Now, what do you want out of me? Fine writing? Do you want masterpieces? Do you want glowing things that can be framed by copywriters? *Or do you want to see the goddamned sales curve stop moving down and start moving up?*

Reeves came up with an idea that would keep his writers' minds focused on what the audience wants, a concept he called the Unique Selling Proposition (often abbreviated to USP). The technique is now taught as part of advertising theory, and it works well for any kind of persuasive communication. The parts of a USP are also some of the ingredients of a good hook:

U is for Unique. A hook should offer something that's not going to be offered by the next hook that comes along or at least offer the same thing in a different way.

S is for Selling. A hook needs a good selling point. Selling points are often confused with benefits, but here's the difference: A benefit is the *change for the better* that your audience will experience if they accept your idea. A selling point is a *reason the benefit will happen.*

P is for Proposition. A proposition is the promise of benefit. Putting the promise of a benefit in your hook is crucial. If your hook can convince your audience that their life will be improved as a result of your idea, your message will sail over the competition, because most people can't—or won't—do this. Even advertising professionals fail most of the time. "Advertising which promises no benefit to the consumer does not sell, yet the majority of campaigns contain no promise whatever," advertising legend David Ogilvy has written, to which he added, "That is the most important sentence in this book. Read it again."

Most business communication isn't as blatant as advertising, but following the precepts of a USP can help ensure audience appeal. It's best to build a USP backwards: start with a proposition (or promise of benefit), then think of its selling points, and, finally, why it's unique. This prevents you from developing unique selling points that lead to a benefit your audience isn't interested in. The three questions to ask, in order, are:

What benefit will your audience get from your idea?
Why will it work?
Why is your way the only way?

The promise of benefit. Assume you're trying to convince Sam that the company's computer system needs updating. If Sam considers himself a forward-thinker, part of your hook might be "A new computer system would show your continuing commitment to the technological improvements you've always been known for." If your suggestion would solve a problem you know he's having, you might say, "A new system means your department would process the order forms in half the time."

The selling points. What proof can you offer that a new computer system will really deliver those benefits? For the first benefit, that Sam will be respected for this decision, you might offer: "Look at Phil in the research department. He updated his equipment, and the president congratulated him on his job." For the second, that order form processing will speed up, you might say, "A friend of mine put in a similar system where he works, and their times have been cut in half."

Uniqueness. What's unique about what you propose? Try to use it to eliminate competing ideas. You might say, "We could simply hire more people, but that would cost much more than the new system. Or we could wait a year for the new computer models to arrive, but we'd still lose more money in the meantime than it would cost us to buy now. Updating the system as soon as possible is the only workable solution."

Reeves summed up a USP as something that "matches a selling point with a consumer benefit and does so in a unique way."

To Receive, Give

The attention you get from an audience is a favor, and favors are exchanged among humans based on a relationship of obligations. If your audience feels they *should* pay attention to you, they are more likely to be open to your ideas. To create obligation, you need to do something for them.

It's not as manipulative as it sounds; after all, exchanging help is the glue that holds society together. The recipe for the glue is in what sociologists call the *rule of reciprocity,* and it is stunningly simple. It states that if I do you a favor, you owe me. It doesn't matter how big or small the favor is, or if you like me or not, or even if you didn't want the favor in the first place. These things make a difference, but they don't change the overall effect.

In one psychology experiment, people in one group were given a free soda by a stranger, while those in another group weren't. When the stranger asked people in both groups to buy raffle tickets, those who had received the soft drink bought twice as many tickets as those who hadn't—even though they had never asked for a soda in the first place. What's more, each ticket cost more than twice what the soda did—yet some people bought seven tickets, just to return the favor. At the end of the experiment, people were asked if they liked the ticket-selling stranger; some did, some didn't. It turned out that how much the seller was liked had no effect on how many tickets people bought. In other words, the force of reciprocity obliterated the force of *likability*, which is itself a powerful heuristic, as we'll see later.

Understanding obligation is a critical prerequisite to casting a hook, because no hook will appeal to an audience that thinks you've taken more than you've given.

We all have reciprocal relationships with many of the people we communicate with. If asked to do someone a favor, most of us will if we can. But to reinforce the rule of reciprocity, you should do two kinds of favors that most people don't bother with: the small and the unrequested.

Small favors have power far beyond their size for several reasons. They show a deeper level of consideration than even big favors do. You would appreciate it if Harry were to give you a ride home from work because your car broke down, but if Jill gives you a ride simply because you didn't want to wait for the carpool, you might appreciate that even more. Harry could hardly have refused, while Jill agreed without a compelling reason.

People impressed with themselves often won't do small favors, because they think it's beneath them. Yet people who succeed at extending their influence know that doing little things for people shows you can put somebody's need before your ego, and that this is a powerful way to set obligation in motion. It was said of Senator Robert Byrd that "if you took out a pencil, he'd sharpen it." Actress Sally Kellerman campaigned for Jerry Brown in his 1992 presidential bid, and when somebody asked her why, she said, "Twenty years ago, I asked ten friends to help me move. He was the only one who showed up." At the time, Jerry Brown was California's secretary of state.

With communication, it's sometimes hard to know who's giving a favor and who's receiving. Imagine Roger and Taja meeting together. Roger might believe he's giving Taja a great gift—his terrific ideas about improving production, and he might expect Taja's gratitude. Meanwhile, Taja feels she's doing him a favor just by listening and offering advice. They may both leave thinking the other is the indebted one.

To avoid this, try to establish a shared give-and-take as soon as possible. In conversational communication, take turns talking. In a presentation, find ways to get your audience (whether it's one person or many) to ask questions, make comments, or challenge what you're saying. If you don't sense reciprocity, don't try to offer a hook. From your audience's point of view, you're still being given the favor of their attention, and offering a hook would only increase their sense of doing something for you.

In written communication to a new audience you can enclose or attach something your audience will perceive as helpful or at least meant to be helpful. Sending them a brochure, as packed with information as it might be, will not be seen as a favor, although enclosing an article they would be interested in may be.

To Give, Receive

Reciprocity is a seesaw of obligations; you can't ride if you don't get on, and if you suddenly hop off, your partner plummets to a hard landing.

This requires that you must also accept favors and the obligations that go with them. When you do, you'll notice another effect of reciprocity: When someone does you one good turn, they want to do you another and then another. Because they've made an investment in you, they want to see their investment pay off and their good judgment confirmed. If it takes another favor to ensure that, they'll give it. The bigger the favor someone does for you, the greater their stake in believing that you were worth it.

All of which means that by either giving favors or getting them, you bind yourself and your audience into a relationship that will influence your communication. The better the relationship, the less time you have to spend on crafting the perfect hook. Your audience will be listening because they feel obligated to.

Use a Lead

People seem to resist the idea that they should get to the essence of their message in a hurry. They offer rationalizations to explain why their case is different. Here are some examples and what's wrong with them:

"I don't want to give away too much of my idea at the beginning so I can build up for a big impressive finish." This is a good idea for a story or a joke but not for persuasive communication. In a story, you hide information to create suspense and set up the surprise ending. That creates uneasiness that in a story is good fun because your listener gets to have a risk-free adventure. In persuasive communication, however, uneasiness is frightening because the risk of accepting a bad idea is real. People won't go along for the ride, because from their point of view you may be headed for a cliff.

"Keeping your audience in the dark and assuming that the conclusion left to the end is going to be more exciting really isn't a productive use of everyone's time," one executive told me. "By having the benefit of the conclusion up front they're better able to understand the context of the discussion in the middle."

"I'll tell him a joke to get him loosened up. Then I'll hit him with my big idea." Making a brief, witty comment may help set a positive mood, but telling a full-scale joke just keeps your audience waiting. The longer the joke, the more impatient your audience is likely to become.

"I need to carefully explain each logical step in sequence so she can see why my conclusion is so brilliant." Important as these steps might have been to you, it's the brilliance your audience wants to hear about. Going into detail about your thought process will be seen as self-serving. What's worse, if your listener doesn't agree that your conclusion is brilliant, she's liable to reject not just that idea but any others you offer.

"I'll tell him all the other people that love my idea, so he'll be favorably inclined before he even hears it." Put yourself in your listener's place. You're hearing about an idea that everyone loves. You're already irritated because, evidently, you're the last to know. And the person you're listening to *still* hasn't told you what it is.

"I'll use this special lettering on the cover of my report. That'll get her attention." This is the printed version of stalling. While it's important to present yourself well on paper, it must be in such a way that draws attention to your *message*, not the presentation.

The Lead

The approaches above don't work because they don't create expectation and interest in what will follow. In journalism, reporters know that the first few sentences of a story—the *lead*—are by far the most important. If any one sentence fails to convince their audience to read the next, then the rest of the story hardly matters.

It's true of business communication as well. "There is no greater sin in business communication than boring somebody," says chemical executive Jack Montgomery. "It's okay in law, but you try not to do it in business."

Whether it's the first sentence of a letter or of a phone conversation, it must create a curiosity or concern that can only be satisfied by continuing to pay attention. Here are six approaches to creating a lead:

The Billboard. How would you get your message noticed by someone speeding by at sixty miles an hour? That's the challenge advertisers face when they write for billboards, one similar to what we now face in today's frantic office. The rule of thumb billboard writers use is to keep their message to seven words or less.

Sometimes a single word can catch and hold attention. As the director of a social services agency, Pat Bowie was having trouble with volunteers. So were others in the coalition Pat's agency belonged to. Some wanted to stop the volunteer program, which would have been a disaster for Pat's agency. Pat was able to head off the threat and get everyone moving in one direction by attaching a clear idea to the trouble. Pat knew it wasn't that the volunteers were irresponsible, lazy, ignorant, or uncooperative, it was just that the agencies all wanted volunteers who could figure out what to do without constantly being instructed. "I found that the key word was *initiative*," she told me, "which represented in everyone's mind a particular concept." Pat used that word in her lead when she spoke to each coalition member.

While reducing your message to seven words won't usually be practical, the attempt can sharpen your focus and will often yield powerful words or phrases, as it did for Pat.

The Bottom Line. The end result of your idea or the final implication of your message is often a good lead, especially if it arouses curiosity or takes people by surprise. If you can make a strong statement such as, "July's figures are half of what they should be," or "I think Javier's the one to head this project," your audience will want to see if you can support your claim.

Sometimes the best lead is expressed in numbers that command attention. "A hook in our business," an assistant treasurer at an international corporation told me, "is very often quantifying the problem. 'I've got a $50 million issue here guys.' That will get their attention." A short list of numbers, rapidly delivered, can be even more effective: "Fergeson's rates are 12 percent cheaper, their approval rating is 16 percent higher, their delivery turnaround is five days instead of ten, and their warranty period is twice as long." Although this lead works well on paper, it's even more impressive in conversation if you can recite figures from memory. The numbers you use should have an immediate impact on your audience. Don't use statistics that you have to explain.

The Headline. The offer of news always creates interest; the more current, the more it will command the attention of your audience. It can be news from inside the company or something outside that affects your business.

In an afternoon meeting, mentioning something new that happened that morning, even if only tangentially connected to your message, can work as a lead. "Jim told me just before lunch," you might say, "that the orders are still coming in at record numbers." Notice that the news quality comes from *when* Jim told you this, not what he said, yet the information seems fresh because Jim said it only hours ago.

The same trick works with news from the outside. "You may have heard," you might begin, "that technology stocks took another major hit in the market this morning," and go on to explain how their continued decline reinforces your message that the information highway is a rocky road and that your company shouldn't immediately jump into producing information on CD-ROM disks.

The Question. "What would happen if the southwest division assembled the product instead of shipping the parts back here to Milwaukee?" Questions that contain a clear scenario that your audience can imagine are especially good leads if your proposal is realistic and specific. Questions such as "How would you like to improve company profits?" sound phony and invite immediate skepticism.

The Handle. When people talk about a new idea, product, or process, they need a fast way to express it, which is what a handle offers. And if a handle is well-constructed, people will repeat it.

Handles are often made by forging two ideas into one. If your suggestion is to build small retail auto supply outlets in strip centers, you might say, "They'll be the 7-Elevens of car parts." If you're suggesting your department add a new position, you might say "Hiring Bob will be like creating our own mini research and development department."

Handles made with superlatives are especially good—if they're true. "Ours will be the first lotion on the market to contain 50 percent guava extract" or "If we get this system, we'll be able to turn around orders faster than anybody in the field." Avoid overblown superlatives, such as *best, finest, highest quality*, or *coolest*. That which can be measured, such as *largest, only*, or *strongest, is more impressive.*

The Sound Bite. Like the snippets we hear on the evening news, a sound bite is a sentence, summary, or anecdote that succinctly condenses a strong feeling into a vivid picture. While a handle is usually a quick way to describe a product or service, a sound bite is usually a quick way to describe a feature or benefit or to make a single point.

Sound bites are especially good when you have a criticism to level or a comment to make in a fast give-and-take meeting. A classic example occurred in the 1988 vice presidential debate, when Lloyd Bentsen used a single sound bite to demolish Dan Quayle, who had compared himself to John F. Kennedy. "Senator," Bentsen said, "I knew Jack Kennedy. Jack Kennedy was a friend of mine. And senator, you're no Jack Kennedy."

A good sound bite will work as a lead because people will want you to follow up on your provocative statement. You can often make a sound bite memorable with humor. Instead of saying "The software is deeply flawed," why not say, "That software's so buggy it comes with a Roach Motel."

A touch of shock value can make a sound bite worth passing on. Don't equivocate. To say "There's some merit to his idea, but we should proceed with caution" would not be a sound bite because it is just too dull. A sound bite would be to say, "His idea is nuts." When Barry Diller, former chair of the Fox television network, wanted to say the network barely survived early criticism, he didn't say "The Fox network faced great challenges when we began." He said, "By the skin of our teeth, we got it going before we got diced."

Techniques for Leads

Any lead will benefit from a few general principles:

Use specifics. Specifics are more believable than generalities. Don't say "I've got a plan to improve profits" if you can say "I've found a new material that will increase profits by 28 percent." If you're writing a report, don't title it "Improving Productivity" if you can title it "Improving Productivity Through Employee Scheduling" or, even better, "Improving Productivity Through the Four-Day Work Week."

Don't use a "blind lead." A blind lead is one in which the benefit or the idea isn't expressed. An example is, "Boss, I've got an idea I think you're really going to get excited about." Because all the information is hidden, the promise of excitement isn't believable, and there is nothing else in the lead to compel interest.

Name your audience. By putting a reference to your audience in your lead, you'll increase interest. If you're talking to Joe in engineering, you might say, "This new form will enable us to get information to engineering much more quickly."

To sum up, a lead must have the following four qualities: it must be interesting, provocative, easy to understand, and brief.

5

Make It Their Idea

No one likes to be bullied. While that seems obvious, some people think that creating a hook means tricking people or forcing them to do something against their will. That's not persuasion, it's coercion.

Arm-twisting and carrot-dangling should be avoided not just because they're unethical but because in the long run, threats and bribes are not effective hooks. What social psychologists have discovered is that if someone is persuaded to do something by threat or bribe, the compliance doesn't stick. Ironically, if the hook you offer is too persuasive, it will eventually fail.

An experiment in social psychology shows how this works. In it, the psychologist visited a group of boys in the second, third, and fourth grades. He brought with him a bag of cheap toys and one enticing toy robot. When he laid out his bounty, he allowed the boys to play with any toy they liked—except the robot. He told them if they touched the forbidden toy they'd be severely punished. When he left the room for a minute, only one of twenty-two boys dared have his way with Mr. Mechanical. Six weeks later, though, when the psychologist's assistant brought the toys back and gave no warning, the boys headed for the robot in droves.

This wasn't a big surprise, but what happened next was. In the researcher's parallel experiment, he presented the toys to another group of boys and simply told them it was *wrong* to play with the robot. Just as with the group that had been threatened, one boy couldn't resist, and the others maintained control. But six weeks later, when the assistant brought the toys back, only seven of the boys would touch the robot.

More than the forbidden-fruit syndrome was at work; after all, the robot was off limits in both cases. What made the difference is how the boys viewed their own decision to stay away. In the first case, the reason for abstaining came clearly from outside: a promise of punishment. In the second case, the children decided what to do based on a piece of advice, not a threat. The difference was whether or not the boys felt that pressure from outside was driving their decision.

This phenomenon explains the quick rise and fall of many a business wunderkind: the new employee who seems to be able to convince everyone to back his projects. His promises are large, his predictions of future calamities without his solutions dire. And although his suggestions get action and may even be effective, he's resented. He may be undermined, even eventually fired, because his communication style removes everyone else's free will. People go along because his reasons seem so powerful that they have no choice. A hook should never be so strong that it's immutable. "I make the decisions of what I am willing to give, and what I am not, ahead of time," says Pat Bowie, "because if you come out looking like you didn't give anything, then it just creates animosity. You may get what you want in that instance, but further down the line it's going to come back at you."

Ask Before You Ask

A good hook isn't pushy. It's an offer, an invitation. Better yet, it's a plan you and your audience create together. Public relations executive Tom Harrison does this by saying to his prospect, "I've got this idea and I want to bounce it off you and get your input to see how you think it's going to be." If the hook fails he finds another; if it succeeds, then Tom needs only to refine it for a later presentation. "By bringing them into it," he says, "then when they need to approve it, they've bought it already."

This works even if your first hook is soundly rejected. In another psychology experiment, researchers found that bargaining hard and then compromising got better results than either starting hard and not budging *or* starting with a reasonable compromise. The reason is that people are more persuaded when they believe something is their own idea—the more they bargain, the more they feel that they've had a hand in the decision.

Tom's technique works well if you can craft your hook ahead of time. But even if you've got to come up with one on the spot, you can bring your audience into the process. Most people aren't shy about telling you what they want, and that can serve as a springboard to your idea.

When Betsy Amster, a literary agent, meets with editors to sell her book ideas, she often begins by asking the editors what projects they're now working on. Next, she might ask what they're looking for. What's important to notice is that by asking, instead of launching into her pitch, she's establishing a give-and-take atmosphere. As she listens to the answers, she makes notes and finds connections between what she's going to offer and what the editor has bought in the past. When it comes time for her to introduce her projects, she may again pose a question. "I see you've done an anthology of coming-of-age stories by Catholic women," she once told an editor. "Would you consider doing one by Jewish women?" she then asked, suggesting an idea the editor eventually bought.

"You've got to stop and say, 'Let's not describe what I'm going to do, but how it's going to affect you,' " says Tom Harrison. Business owner Scott Ray agrees. "You have to start by saying 'Let's not put me on stage here, let's put you on stage,' " he says.

Find and Follow Agreement

Once you find out what your audience values and wants, you should agree with some part of it and build from there. Don't introduce your idea by saying something like, "I can see how that worked in the past, but times have changed. My idea's much better." Even mild confrontation puts you on opposing sides instead of uniting you and your audience as a team. Your audience will see you as trying to sell something different than what they're used to. Instead of doing what social marketers call *channeling existing behavior patterns,* which is relatively easy, you'll be trying to create *new behavior patterns*, which is nearly impossible.

This doesn't mean you need to change your idea—only your hook. The way to do it is to *find and follow agreement*. Look first for major points to agree on; it you find these, then directly state your agreement before you offer your suggestion. ("That is my philosophy, too. Let me show you how my idea fits in.") Your audience has given you your hook; after all, it's their philosophy.

If you're having trouble finding anything you feel you can agree with, continue to ask your audience questions and mentally break down their answers into components. You will often find that you can agree with an abstract concept if not a specific plan of action. Listen for these features in what your audience is saying:

Motivation. Deep in your audience's id, there may be an overriding emotion that's driving them. Perhaps the person you're listening to is afraid of a particular competitor. You may think that competitor is really no threat, but you can still identify with what it feels like to fear competition, and you can agree with that. "I remember when I had Hoffman Industries breathing down my neck," you might say. "I can understand what you're going through, and I agree it calls for some kind of action." From there, you can suggest the action.

Or the person might be trying to act like an expert when she clearly isn't. The desire to be knowledgeable may be what's motivating her, and that's a value most of us would agree is good. You might support her by saying, "I also think that we need to know as much as we can about the situation before we try anything new. Here is the result of my research and my thinking."

Method. Although the idea you're pitching might be unlike anything your audience has done, you may have some methods in common. Perhaps she has all her ideas reviewed by a trusted group of coworkers. If you do the same, tell her. "I had a lot of input on this idea from Cheryl in marketing and Rick in product development." Tell her how your coworkers helped, and point out the similarities in your methods of working.

Goals. Listen to what your audience is saying about the ultimate goals they have for a particular project or even for their job in general. Ultimately, we all have the same goal: to spend time on this earth in a way that we believe is worthwhile. Obviously, you need to be more specific than that, but somewhere between what you want and what your audience wants, there is probably a general statement on which you can agree.

Sometimes you can hone in on specific goals by narrowing down larger ones. If your audience seems to have quality customer service as a general goal, try to find out what they think that entails. Does it mean improving product design according to customer suggestions or servicing customers after they buy the product? After you have determined a few of your audience's specific goals, you can pick the one that's closest to your own goals and offer your agreement.

Results. Though closely linked to goals, results are a bit different. I think of goals as unquantifiable qualities: improved performance, better value, enhanced reputation. Results are the measurements you believe show that you're either achieving or not achieving your goal: the number of customers served in a given time, the specifications of a product compared to its cost, the number of times company experts are quoted by the media. If you can't agree about anything else, you might be able to see that at least the results your audience is trying to achieve are worthy.

"I think you're right, C.J. We've got to get those numbers up. Here's why I think my idea will help."

Don't Be a Yes-Person

After encouraging you to agree with your audience, I want to emphasize that I'm not suggesting you fake agreement. Fooling someone is usually harder than it looks, and your true feelings are bound to come out eventually. Keep in mind the principle: *Find* and follow agreement. By finding genuine agreement in the first place, and moving in that direction, you're less likely to talk about things you don't agree on, and more likely to come across one mutually agreeable point after another. After agreement, as you introduce your idea into the conversation, you both will tend to seek similarities in your views instead of dissimilarities. "If you're both going along in the same direction," says business owner Scott Ray, "and one of you turns and gives the other a tug, it's much more likely they'll make that little adjustment."

If you typically pause between chapters when reading a book, you might want to make an exception here, because I have some news to tell you in the next chapter.

It's New!

Did you finish the last chapter and turn immediately to this one? If so, then you see the power of a hook that states or implies something new. The appeal of something new is practically impossible for people to resist. Step into any office and ask, "Have you heard the news?" and you will be guaranteed instant attention nine times out of ten. Advertisements with news in them are recalled by 22 percent more people than ones without news. News is so important in the world of advertising that adman David Ogilvy has a simple prescription for copywriters who have news to tell but leave it out of their ads: "They should be boiled in oil." The same might be said of business communicators who are shy about expressing the newsworthiness of their messages.

Certain words and phrases imply news: *now*, *just arrived*, *just discovered*, *suddenly*, *introducing*, *the first*, and *advanced*. News often hides deep within the details of a message. If you recently received information that affects what you have to say, you can begin with, "I just got this from Tony, and it's going to change the numbers." If you've changed your mind about something, you can say, "I suddenly realized we don't have to hire Skyrocket Consulting. We can figure this out ourselves." Any transition from one process to another can be news. "Well, the last of the mailers just went out," you might announce. "And I have some suggestions about the next phase."

To find news, look for difference. Not just the difference between the past and the present, which is an obvious clue to news, but any difference. If your function or knowledge is substantially different from that of the person you're communicating with, something you've known for years may be news to them. "Let me introduce some concepts we use in research to make these kinds of decisions," you might say.

If you know your message is going to sound like the same old thing even though it isn't, emphasizing the difference between what your audience expects and what you're going to deliver can help your hook. Adding the phrase, "it's not what you might think," can add interest by starting an internal questioning process in the audience. Hearing the phrase, Sam begins to ask himself, "What might I think? And how might this be different? Will it be different from the difference I think I would think?" He'll be interested in finding out the answer.

Something old can also be new. If you're returning to a previous way of doing things, the change is news. If you're sticking to a particular method while everyone else is changing, you can say,

"We've made a new commitment to continue our traditional method, which we believe is superior."

Hollywood describes any movie that features a character who's been thrust into an unfamiliar situation as a "fish out of water" story, like E.T. in suburbia or Lawrence in Arabia. It's new and interesting to see familiar people or places combined with unfamiliar people or places—and the same goes for ideas. An old idea in a new context is news. When Jerry Brown was running for president, he attracted attention by announcing his toll-free campaign-contribution hotline. Having a toll-free number is, in itself, not a new idea, but someone on Brown's team realized it was new in the context of politics.

7

It's Free!

Have you ever stopped to think about the phrase *free gift?* Or *complimentary gift?* Or *no-cost gift?* They are all redundant statements in that they offer to give a free thing for free.

People love the idea of getting something for nothing so much that advertisers often pack the idea of free into every word they can. And there are a number of ways you can build the appeal of something free into your hook without giving things away.

One technique is to express your benefit as a bonus, like this: "Using my plan, it's as if we were getting five hours of computer time free." In another case, you might say your idea will "free up" hours for other needs. Or you can say you can improve production, "at no cost." Since most good ideas in business generate or save time or money, putting an idea to work can often be seen as getting something "for free."

Another idea that's closely associated with "free" is "freedom." For most people, the more choices, the better. You may be able to create a hook by putting your message in terms of freedom, as in, "this will give us the freedom to buy now and pay later," or "that decision will limit our freedom to operate in the future."

Actually giving someone something for free can, of course, also work as a powerful hook because it combines two heuristics. The first is the feeling of greater freedom, since having something gives someone more possible choices than not having it; they can choose to keep it or throw it away. The second heuristic is reciprocity. As we saw earlier, if you give someone something, they feel an obligation to do something for you.

It's Easy!

Similar to the hook of freedom is the hook of ease, because if something is easier to do, that means you've got the freedom to spend the time and effort you've saved elsewhere. Claiming something is easier than something else, or easier than it was before, is a powerful hook, as you might guess from how often it appears in advertising.

In business, the words "effective" and "efficient" have become near synonyms for "easy." So if your message will in any way increase the ease, efficiency, or effectiveness of your audience, you have the heart of a hook. The important part of this hook is the details. The more specific you can be about how much easier your idea will make things, by reducing hours or energy, for example, the better.

You can also use an easy hook not only for your idea but as an inducement to agree, no matter what your idea is. After hard bargaining, you might say, "Let's make this easy on everybody and try this."

It's Unavailable!

If the promise of news is a powerful way to hold attention, so is the promise of no news. What do I mean by that? I'm sorry, I can't tell you. It's a secret.

If you find that now you *really* want to know what I'm talking about, you've felt the influence of what social psychologists call the effect of *scarcity*. Studies show that we automatically see something that's scarce as more valuable, regardless of whether we know anything else about it. One theory explains this by noting that scarcity restricts our freedom, which challenges our survival, so we react by wanting the scarce item more than before.

In one experiment, a company selling wholesale beef to supermarket buyers gave its customers one of three pitches. The first pitch said, this is great beef, you should buy a lot. The second said, this is great beef, and by the way we're running out—next month we probably won't have any. And the third said, this is great beef, but—and I'm not supposed to tell you this—we're running out and next month we probably won't have any.

Customers in the second group, who thought the beef was going to be scarce, bought twice as much as the first group. The third group, who thought not only the beef, but the *information itself*, was scarce, bought *six times* as much beef as the first group.

The scarcity effect is a hidden hook in all kinds of situations. It goes beyond the "three-day sale" and "limited quantities" warnings we're used to ignoring in popular advertising. Scarcity is why conspiracy theories are so attractive: the "suppressed" information that's revealed automatically seems valuable because it was formerly secret. Scarcity drives rumor, which is "forbidden" information. Scarcity is why people suppose that private meetings must involve especially interesting topics.

Studies show that when information is unavailable, people think that it's not only more desirable but that it's more accurate, *even if they don't know what it is*. When students at one university were told that a speech against coed dorms would be banned, opposition to coed dorms rose even though no one had heard the speech. In another case, researchers ran several mock trials to see what happens when juries are told to ignore information. What they found was this: Use a piece of information as normal, admissible evidence, and the jury awards a certain amount of money. Have the judge tell the next jury to ignore the same information, and the jury will award *more* money.

Since the scarcity effect can create so many layers of influence, crafting a hook with it takes care. Here is a sampling of the dynamics of scarcity applied to five common commodities:

Time. A deadline raises the importance of something, which is why almost all persuasive communication should have one attached. Whenever you have a legitimate time frame, make sure to emphasize it. If you don't, create one, based on your own preference: "I'll need to hear from you on this no later than Thursday, so I can complete my planning."

Even more compelling is a project whose deadline has passed but that can be revived. If you've been given a deadline by someone who you know can be adjusted, you can nonetheless use the original deadline to add appeal to your proposition. "Tom told me he had to have a decision by yesterday," you might say, "but if we get our offer to him today, I think he'll still go for the deal."

A person's availability affects how important they seem. If you want to hire Mr. Cramer as a consultant and tell your boss that Cramer has plenty of time to devote to your company, you've just made him sound less than special. If he's so good, why isn't he busy?

Notice that scarcity depends on the uniqueness of something, and that can affect how deadlines work. If you offer Samantha something with a deadline attached, and Paul has the exact same offer without a deadline, then your offer is *less* desirable. It's the perceived restriction of freedom that makes the scarcity effect work. If the offers are truly the same, then Samantha will choose the offer that doesn't restrict her freedom—in this case, to decide at a later date.

If you're offering advice to someone who has to make a decision before a deadline, your hook should always offer more freedom, no matter what you're advising. The argument for accepting the offer would be something like "We should take this offer while we can. It might not be an option later." That emphasizes future restrictions and makes acceptance seem more desirable. The argument for rejecting the offer might be "I think we shouldn't tie ourselves down right now. We should keep our options open." That emphasizes maintaining the present freedom.

Quantity. By definition, a little of something is scarcer than a lot of something, and a "one-of-a-kind" item is rarest of all. Even when an option is completely unavailable, it affects decisions. Psychologists call this the influence of the *phantom choice*. Suddenly, whatever features the phantom choice had, those are the ones we want. You can build a hook using the effect of a phantom choice by pointing out a missed opportunity or unavailable product that's like the idea you're proposing. "This is exactly like the Thompson deal we missed out on last year," you might say, then detail the similarities.

In trying to emphasize the uniqueness of something, people often resort to unbelievable claims that put them on the wrong side of the scarcity principle. "It's the only solution that will work," you'll hear Max say, which, unless it's backed up with solid reasons, Karen will dismiss as balderdash. Once that happens, the scarcity principle begins to work *against* Max. Suddenly, all those other unspoken (and therefore scarce) solutions seem attractive to Karen.

Money. The scarcity principle is what makes more expensive things seem better. The more something costs, the further it's removed from easy access—a restriction of freedom. That's why a low price by itself is not an effective hook. To make a low price attractive, it must seem to be a bargain—something available now for a lower price than it would be at a later time. That raises the threat of a future restriction of freedom: "If I don't get this now, I might have to pay a higher price later."

You might think that if something inexpensive seems less desirable than something pricey, then something free must seem worthless, which would seem to contradict the "free" hook discussed earlier. The key here is *perceived value*. If Raymond thinks there's any value at all attached to the free item, then he'll want it, because not having it—and not being able to get it later—would make it scarce. Better to get it now and not take any chances.

Loyalty. An alliance you can depend on is a rare thing and often hard to be sure of, which is why loyalty (or the threat of losing it) is particularly seductive in a scarcity hook. "We've built a rapport with Spencer Industries," you might say. "It would be a shame to threaten it for this one deal." In addition to alluding to others' loyalty, you can always bring your own into play, either positively or negatively. "If we have an attitude of mutual support, we can get it done" or "I've always backed you, Tom, but I can't go along with this one."

Information. If you have special knowledge, an inside track, a little-known fact, or an overlooked feature as part of your message, you've got a scarcity hook. If people holding an opinion contrary to yours are hiding issues, revealing those issues will make them seem more important than they might otherwise be. Even if your information is the result of routine research, using words that have some connotation of secrecy can help interest your audience. "I took a closer look at the problem," you might say, "and I think I saw some things that everybody else is trying to sweep under the carpet." If you're having a one-on-one meeting in someone's office, just asking them to close the door for privacy will increase your listener's interest.

You can also turn secrecy against your opponents by suggesting that their information won't stand scrutiny. "I'm not sure what they're afraid of," you may begin. "I just want to get everything out on the table." That hook implies that there is undisclosed information, and because of the scarcity principle, it will seem true, even though no one knows what it is.

Even if you're not going to use a hook based on scarcity, you've got to watch out for its effects. Sometimes the impression of secrecy can come out of nowhere and ruin your communication. Pat Bowie found this out when she tried to work out an agreement between several people over the phone. Even though she'd tell Chris everything that Barbara said, Chris immediately suspected that something was left out—the appeal of unavailable information. And so it went with each person she called. "What it looked like was that I was playing fast and loose with everybody," she said. "And that's when it hit me that when it comes to the real critical, difficult decisions, it's best to do them face-to-face. Everybody's at the table, and then everybody has to deal with what they're saying. There's no hidden agenda—or there may be a hidden agenda, but at least everybody is at the table dealing with it all at once."

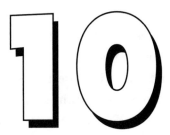

Don't Lose Out

People hate to lose something even more than they like to get something of the same value—another effect of the scarcity principle. Getting something represents acquiring freedom, which is a step forward. If you don't get it, then at least you're in the same spot. But if you lose it, you've fallen behind. Hooks that offer to protect your audience from loss are often stronger than hooks that offer gain.

Experiments have borne this out. In one, a brochure urging young women to practice self-examination for breast cancer was tested with two different headlines. The first was, "You can lose several potential health benefits by failing to spend only 5 minutes each month doing breast self-examination." The second was, "You can gain several potential health benefits by spending only 5 minutes each month doing breast self-examination." The first headline was significantly more successful.

It's often easy to emphasize loss-protection by switching a proposal from positive to negative. For example, if you're suggesting that your company should advertise on the Internet, instead of talking about the customers you'll gain, emphasize the customers you would otherwise lose to your Internet-advertising competitors. You can often use this hook in conversations. Instead of saying, "If we fax this to him before Friday, there's a good chance he'll look at our proposal," you can emphasize loss-protection by saying, "If we don't fax this to him by Friday, there's no way he'll look at our proposal."

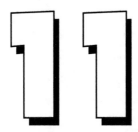

Feeding Frenzy

When scarcity is combined with rivalry, the appeal of an idea or item seems to multiply exponentially. It's the kind of appeal that fueled California's real estate boom in the 1980s—dozens of buyers would fight over a single house, driving the price of bungalows beyond the half-million dollar mark.

It's a scenario that's not limited to home buyers. The scarcity-rivalry hook can drive up stock prices and inflate movie star salaries. "When people get irrational is when things get interesting," a real estate agent told me. The hook may work because it triggers some ancient biological instinct in us to compete for scarce resources.

But you don't have to create a bidding war or stage an auction to use it. Jack Montgomery, the chemical executive, used a scarcity-rivalry hook to improve communication at a product update briefing, normally a tedious affair, where a presenter describes the technical specifications of raw plastic resins to a group of sales representatives. Since Jack knew that sales reps tend to be naturally competitive, Jack decided that instead of *offering* the information, he would *conceal* it, and let the reps compete to draw it out. Jack turned his presentation into a game he called "Name That Resin," during which he held up a product made from the resin and asked questions. "You had to guess what the material was," Jack recalled. "Then you had to give me three reasons why this particular material was the one to use." Winners would get a prize.

The reps, eager to show off their expertise, clamored to be first with the right answers. When Jack held up the last product, the frenzy kicked into high gear, with answer after answer turning out wrong. The reason was that Jack had thrown in a ringer. The last product was a prototype manufactured from a brand-new resin, as yet unreleased. With the audience all ears, Jack delivered his most important message—the introduction of a new product.

Although Jack created this hook intuitively, he used both rivalry and scarcity effectively. Jack knew that rivalry would work as a lure, because sales reps are so attuned to competing for customers. To that he added scarce items—prizes for winning and the admiration that comes with demonstrating expertise. But look at another effect of scarcity in this example: by making the *answers* scarce—the very information he wanted to communicate—he boosted the perceived desirability and accuracy of that information. And the reps enjoyed the process. "They loved it," he recalled. "I had all the managers walk up to me multiple times and tell me how wonderful this was."

A group setting is a natural place to use the scarcity-rivalry hook, but there are many subtler ways than staging a mock game show. In a meeting, you may not want to have people actually compete to answer a question, yet you can create a similar feel with a simple technique. First make a statement without revealing specifics: "Profits in our glider division are up." And then follow it with a question that *invites* rivalry: "Would anyone care to guess by how much?" Whether anyone offers an answer or you treat the question as rhetorical and answer it yourself, the effect is the same: The sense of sudden rivalry will boost the interest in what you're saying. In its more basic form, your hook may simply allude to competition, as in the phrase, "Here's a bit of information I'll bet our competitors would like to have."

12

What Your Package Says

There's a joke recounted by Joseph Telushkin that goes like this: A Jewish woman is wheeling her grandson in a baby carriage. A woman stops her and says, "What a beautiful baby!" "Ah, this is nothing!" replies the proud grandmother. "You should see his pictures."

Now consider the case of an experiment done by consumer researcher Richard Feinberg. He put a group of college students in a room and asked them to give to charity. A third did. Then he put another group in an identical room with one exception: a MasterCard credit card symbol was present. This time, almost 90 percent made a donation. And not because they could use a MasterCard to make the donation—that wasn't part of the experiment. In fact, nothing was mentioned about the symbol.

Apparently just the presence of the symbol influenced the students to feel freer with their money.

Both the Jewish grandma and the free-spending students responded unconsciously to the power of a two-dimensional image. It's this unconscious response we have to visual cues that drives corporations to spend millions to blanket the world with their logos. And while you don't need to become a graphic designer to take advantage of this effect, it's important to understand some of the visual aspects of persuasion.

First Impressions

The look of business documents actually has two effects. The first is its initial impact. That is part of its hook and what I'll be describing in this section. The second is a deeper impression—one that comes from reading. I'll talk about that later, in the spin section of the book.

The first impression we get from any document comes from its overall visual form. That is, the style of your letterhead is not the first thing your audience will notice. The visual hook is on the macro level: This is a letter, as opposed to a brochure, a memo, a newsletter, or a ransom note. That overall form communicates something—It's more personal than an advertising flyer, less personal than a hand-written invitation. Let's take a look at these macro connotations:

Memos. Memos are all business. Before faxes, e-mail, and the rest, this was the document that said "Here's a quick summary of where things stand." The form of a memo implies that it didn't take long to write and that the information in it is subject to change. Memos usually don't have much warmth, so it's not a good form for a thank-you, for example. A letter is better.

Letters. Letters can run the gamut from being warm and open to cold and distant, even threatening. In spite of this, they do have a personal connotation: They are almost always directed at one person, whereas a memo or report can go to a crowd.

Handwritten notes. Handwriting carries the direct feeling of the person writing. It's essential for thank-you notes or "thought you'd be interested" notes attached to articles, but long handwritten business letters seem amateurish. Handwriting on a typewritten document can make its message seem more immediate, as if you only had time to scribble your reaction and send it along.

Reports. The report form has an air of academia that surrounds it. A report is assumed to be researched, contain objective information that will stay accurate for some time, and require study. A six-page report, for example, won't seem as quick a read as a six-page memo—even if it contains exactly the same information. That means a reader might set a report aside and never read it, or it may mean that when she does read it, she'll give it her full attention. The payoff for taking the risk to produce a report instead of a memo or letter is that because the reader gives it more attention, she'll be more inclined to believe what it says. This is a function of the heuristic of *consistency*; in effect, the reader's internal conversation is, "Since I'm devoting more time to this, it must be for a good reason."

Brochures. A brochure is advertising, and all advertising is suspect. There's nothing personal about it, and there's nothing unbiased about it, which is why many brochures produced by budding desktop publishers fail to influence anyone. As far as a visual hook, many of these would be better off if they were converted to letters or reports.

Convincing brochures are usually expensive, because the best hook they can deliver is one that says, "My company is so successful we can afford to send you this beautiful brochure." Even these should be used carefully. Although Tom Harrison's company has fancy brochures, they don't always use them. "We have to know our audience," says Tom. For some clients, Tom knows that "If we go in with a flashy brochure and a flashy presentation, they're going to think we're too expensive. It's going to intimidate them, and they're not going to want to work with us."

Flyers. A flyer is a one-page loose advertisement. The connotation it has is some urgency and a little desperation. In business, it's seldom good for more than advertising specials at trade shows or getting people to the company picnic. The exception is retail advertising, which is another subject.

Catalogs. The catalog used to be a musty form, one preferred by shut-ins. That all changed with companies like L. L. Bean, J. Crew, and Patagonia. A good catalog now can carry more warmth, integrity, and trustworthiness than many love letters.

Newsletters. Newsletters used to *be* letters—they looked typewritten, and good ones had a reputation for being up-to-the-minute and filled with essential information. Now, most look like mini-newspapers—three columns filled with stylish layouts and good photos. They may have some of the connotations of journalism: They seem objective, timely, and filled with news, but more often (because there are so many these days) those effects have worn thin, and they seem to be what they are: propaganda.

Magazines. Magazines are perceived to be more authoritative than newsletters or newspapers. In general, they're seen as more opinionated but more in-depth.

Books. A book is still the wizened old professor of printed publications. Anything in book form will be seen as more accurate and authoritative than something in a letter, brochure, newsletter, or magazine. It's an ancient reaction of ours, and not one that will disappear soon, in spite of the Internet. The more bookish a publication is (book-size instead of magazine-size; thick instead of thin; hard-cover instead of paper; from an established publisher instead of a company) the more weight it will carry. For some reason—perhaps because a book is usually the work of one author—a book can be both objective and personal at the same time.

E-Mail. One of the newest two-dimensional forms of communication is e-mail, which has connotations that are still forming. It's been called immediate, personal, and casual, more like a printed phone call than written information. Jack Montgomery uses e-mail extensively within his company, but he seldom sends it to people outside. "I don't like the fact that it goes out in DOS format, that it looks crude," he told me. "I don't like the whole sense of it, the confusing address. I don't think that's appropriate for customers." Jack points out that you can't sign the bottom of an e-mail, and he believes that touch of personal commitment makes a big difference. (I'll have more to say about e-mail in the spin section of this book.)

Faxes. Another form with uncertain connotations, faxes are best used as a supplement to other communications and, even then, are best kept between friends. Pat Bowie comments:

I only fax to people I have an ongoing relationship with. And if it's something they need to see. If it's a complicated thing that, over the phone, nobody's going to get or if it's information

I want them to read, I'll just fax it. I'll usually even call, or have someone on my staff call, to say "we're going to be faxing this over," so that they know it's coming. Because a lot of people get so many faxes they don't even read them. I know with me, I will take a pile of faxes and I may not read them until the end of the day. If I've expected it, I pick it up right away, I read it right away, if somebody tells me, "oh, by the way, I'm faxing you something," then I will look for it, I'll get it, and I'll read it. So I only use the fax in conjunction with the phone, even if it's "Oh, by the way, I need to fax you this, will you please look at it give me a call or fax me back.

Jack Montgomery points out that the look of this new paper trail can create problems that only surface later:

In terms of documentation, if someone comes back to review documents in a crisis or contentious situation, a collection of faxes or sloppy, casual-looking communications implies a casualness with fact—even if that isn't the case. If the documentation looks crisp and professional, it adds to the sense of credibility. This is pretty damn important when people are under the gun.

Obviously, day-to-day communication can only be stretched so far to give it the hook of a particular form: You can't make a memo into a book just because you want it to be authoritative. But you can often change a brochure into a letter or a memo into a report. The point is to think about the form before you fire off a particular message.

Combining Hooks

One day Tom Harrison received a call from a colleague at another public relations agency who said she had heard that one of Tom's clients was going to leave his agency. She told Tom that if he could save his account, he should do it. If not, she asked if she could be the first to know so she could beat the competition and, perhaps, win the account for her agency.

The effect of this news on Tom was electric. He worked very hard to save the account, which he did, and he was eternally grateful to his competitor who had tipped him off. Throughout the years he's returned the favor many times over.

At first glance, Tom's colleague might seem to have been foolish. After all, knowing that her competitor was in a weak position, she could have approached his client directly for their business. However, that might have made her seem conniving to her potential client. She realized that instead of trying to create a shaky hook for the client, she had the chance to craft a terrific hook for Tom, her rival. In fact, she was able to combine three hooks into one. Let's look at how it worked and what she got from it.

First, she saw that the scarcity hook applied to her information. She knew that its rarity boosted its believability and importance, and, since she was the source, it boosted her importance, too.

Second, she saw that the information contained a rivalry hook, since Tom would suddenly be competing for the account.

And last, she engaged a reciprocity hook because telling him all this was a favor, which would someday need to be returned.

She was now poised to win no matter what happened. If Tom had discovered he couldn't save the account, he would tell her the moment the client was in play, giving her a crucial advantage. If Tom saved the account, he would still think of her as important (having helped him save an extra-important client) and would owe her a favor.

It's natural that some appeals will have more than one hook, and these can be very powerful. If you're lucky enough to find one, use it. But don't go out of your way to try to combine several hooks into one message. You only need one good hook to pull in your audience, and once that's done, a hook's job is over. If you continue to try to hook somebody after they're already interested you run the risk of loosing your prospect.

Jan Baird, a marketing consultant, notes that you can't let all the hard work you've put into a hook blind you to what your audience is thinking. "If we're really passionate about what we're saying, as many people are who are trying to persuade," she told me, "we can just get so absorbed in our passion that we completely lose track of what the other person is thinking." She recalled a time when a hook was taken so fast, the other member of her team didn't even realize it. He wanted to keep pitching:

I've been working with the state in promoting doing business in California, and we've been asking companies for a significant financial investment in the program, and mostly meeting with CEOs. Everyone is so different. And they come at projects like this differently.

We had a stock presentation, and we ran into a CEO personality, and he just said, "What do you want? Okay." He didn't want to see the pitch. That wasn't why he was buying in. He was buying in because the governor's office was there. We didn't need to sell. We didn't even need to describe it.

Yet the advertising executive Jan was with wanted to go on, showing his ad layouts, media plan, and strategy. It was unnecessary, and Jan had to cut things off by saying "Thank you very much!" before they hit something the CEO wouldn't like. For them, the process ended with the hook; they never even got to spin, although we will get to it next.

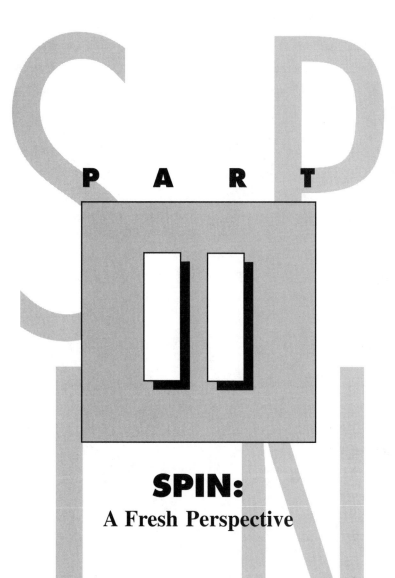

P A R T

II

SPIN:
A Fresh Perspective

If a hook gets people to bite, spin is what reels them in. "Spin at its most positive," one executive told me, "is finding a perspective someone else hadn't considered."

Offering your perspective is essential even when you think the reasons behind your request, plan, or idea are perfectly obvious. That's because by explaining, you're communicating something else: that you think the person is entitled to an explanation. Your audience will identify with your effort to reason and move toward a goal even if your *particular* reasons don't make much sense to them.

You can see the effect in an experiment in which a researcher tried to cut into a long line of people waiting to use a copy machine. When she said, "Excuse me, I have five pages. May I use the Xerox machine?" 60 percent of the people she asked allowed her to move ahead in the line. When she offered an explanation, she got a much better response. By saying, "Excuse me, I have five pages. May I use the Xerox machine *because I'm in a rush?*" 94 percent of those she asked let her in. What's amazing is that when she offered an explanation that didn't add any information, she got a nearly identical response. When she said, "Excuse me, I have five pages. May I use the Xerox machine *because I have to make some copies?*" 93 percent of the people complied. Her statement had no content, but it had spin; it offered her perspective. Any explanation will have spin, but the art of spin is recognizing and expressing your perspective as effectively as possible.

Although many people think spin is a brand-new black art practiced by unscrupulous politicians, it is actually an ancient and respected craft. The Greeks invented it about 2,500 years ago, called it rhetoric, and thought everyone should learn it to be considered educated. Aristotle, who defined rhetoric as "the art of discovering all the possible means of persuasion on any subject whatsoever," was one of the world's first spin doctors, and was rather good at it—he advised a successful politician of the time known as Alexander the Great.

Aristotle divided rhetoric into three general areas: methods that throw a favorable light on the source of your information (either you or someone you cite); methods that soften up the audience and make them want to accept your message; and methods that demonstrate or prove your ideas. In this part of the book, we'll approach spin the same way, beginning with techniques to boost your credibility, such as citing an expert; then we'll move on to those that soften your audience, such as conceding on a point; and finally, to techniques such as stories, metaphors, and labels that demonstrate your argument.

Spin usually comes after your hook, and, unlike a hook, isn't necessarily short or even easy to understand. It depends entirely on your subject and your audience. You might concentrate on one long, elaborately developed spin—perhaps the story of your company and its rise to eminence in its field—or you might jump from spin to spin, sealing doubts until your argument is airtight.

Spin can also become your hook, usually when you're countering an opinion. In that case, the lead of the hook is something such as "It's not what you think—in fact, it's the complete opposite," after which the spin must quickly move in to prove it. That's the most common hook made from spin, but any spin can become a hook if your audience is particularly receptive to it.

Spin generally works in two steps: you establish the criteria by which you want your information to be evaluated, and you meet that criteria with the points you make. The idea is to show your audience one view and eliminate their tendency to look elsewhere.

In spin that pumps up your credibility, you highlight your experience, credentials, and good character to corroborate your claim or those of the source you're using. Your experience and credentials tend to show that you know what you're talking about. Your character comes into play because if people like you, they trust that you won't steer them wrong. The experience, credentials, and character of your source can help reinforce your opinion.

Spin that seeks to make your audience receptive is more subtle. It's based not on the merits of your argument but on human nature. For example, in the spin I call *Give In to Win*, a concession on your part triggers a feeling in your audience that they should also compromise. You gently shift the criteria for agreement from "What are the facts?" to "What is a fair way for us to solve this together?"

Spin that demonstrates your ideas is what most of us think of as making a case. Using a metaphor or analogy is probably the most common, as when you say, "We all saw that the paperless office never came to pass. It'll be the same way with the information superhighway." Another method is showing causation: "When Heritage Industries switched to this method, their production rose by 22 percent."

The chapters that follow give you the particulars of these themes—establishing authority, softening your audience, and demonstrating your points. Remember, though, that no matter what kind of spin you use, to be effective it must come naturally from your argument. "I think spin can be very useful, can be very smart, can save people time," says marketing consultant Jan Baird, "if you simply point out the aspect of whatever it is you're talking about that they'd be interested in. *That's* spin."

Join Your Audience

It's been said that for 99 percent of the time that human beings have existed, we've lived together in groups of no more than thirty-five people. In other words, for several million years, our species has evolved a set of beliefs and feelings based on being part of a small tribe. The past few thousand years of living in larger groups has done little to change that.

The effect on our communication is easy to guess: We believe what comes from us, and we don't believe what comes from them—regardless of who us and them are. Research psychologists have found that we believe people who are similar to us, whether that similarity has anything to do with the issue at hand or not. We trust people who have dark hair like us, wear business suits like we do, follow the Chicago Bulls, claim Philly as a hometown, read

Wired, drink cappuccino, or ski. In experiments, groups of people were divided simply on the basis of a coin toss. Yet when they were questioned about people in their own group as compared to people in the other group, they reported *their* people to be more likable, to have better personalities, and to be more productive.

Getting to "Us"

The tendency we have to trust our own means that convincing someone (or even getting them to listen to you) often has little to do with what you're saying but everything to do with who you are. If you can show you have something in common with your audience, then you're that much closer to being considered part of their group. Jan Baird always looks for the personal connection. "You link it to something that is really near and dear to that person's heart," she told me. "I was just talking to somebody this morning who's presenting a public affairs program that I've designed to the final corporate person. I said, 'So what's this person into in their personal life? Does he go to a church, is he involved in Boy Scouts, are his kids in soccer, does he coach a team, does he like to fly, is there anything about him that will help me further define this program or highlight something in the program that he'll connect with?' "

Even better is a relationship that's developed over time. "I have found out the hard way," says public relations executive Tom Harrison, "that doing good work is important, but you can do good work all day long and still lose clients if you don't have the relationship, too."

The tribal effect means that we're influenced most by the people we see most. In one psychology experiment, faces were flashed on a screen so fast that the subjects couldn't remember which ones they'd seen and which ones they hadn't. Yet when the subjects met the people pictured in person, they liked the ones whose pictures had been flashed the most—and they were more persuaded by them. For that reason, just making your face familiar will help you become more persuasive. A financial officer explained to me how his company works to make the Wall Street crowd part of their tribe:

> Our company has received awards year in and year out for the quality of its investor relations program. What's made it successful is that we are religious in every year going to New York and putting on a very large, all-day kind of presentation . . . Another part of it is just the frequency with which we communicate with the people. We go on regular tours. In addition to the one big presentation in New York, we're visiting these people usually at a minimum four times a year, so after each quarter, there will be quarterly tours, where they'll go around and actually meet in smaller, one-on-ones, or ten-on-ones.

Judging whether someone is "like you" or "one of them" isn't usually triggered by a single similarity; instead, it is an accumulation of similarities, the gestalt of a person. Each part is a clue, and the whole is greater than the sum of its parts. Some of those parts are:

Clothing. The research done by social psychologists shows where the "dress for success" rule of thumb goes wrong: What's impressive to one group isn't necessarily so to another. In one experiment, people asked strangers for money to make a phone call. Researchers found that when the requester's clothing matched the stranger's, they got their money more than two thirds of the time. When the clothing didn't match, more than half of the strangers turned them down.

To be persuasive, then, the answer isn't to always wear a power suit but to match your audience. If you're going to another company to make a presentation or just meet with someone, think about what the people there wore the last time you were there. If you've never been there, you can do what energy consultant Ed Seider often does: He calls the receptionist and simply asks what attire would be appropriate. Ed learned this after showing up too many times wearing a business suit only to find he needed to convince engineers who had just come in from the oil fields wearing jeans and hard hats. To them, Ed's suit was a subtle sign that he didn't have the practical experience to know what he was talking about, which, of course, he did. That didn't mean he arrived in oil-stained overalls. He just wore a sports shirt and left his tie at home.

When you can't plan ahead, at least think ahead. If you're wearing a business suit—either the male or female version—and you're called from your office to attend a meeting, consider whether you should show up wearing your jacket or not. That simple change can make a big difference. Wearing a suit coat in a brainstorming meeting will tend to make you (and, by association, your ideas) seem stuffy and conformist. Appear coatless with your sleeves rolled up, and you'll look ready to let the ideas fly and to do the hard job of making them work. Or, if your jacket's off and you're called to a meeting, you may want to put it on to increase the signal of authority.

If your office has a casual day, that's not necessarily a time to wear what you do on the weekends. If your dress strays too far from the social norm at your office, coworkers will feel they've seen another side of you—one that might cast doubts on your full loyalty to the tribe.

Language. Tribes develop dialects—more efficient, specialized ways to pass information. The result is not only faster communication, but communication that seems truer because it's more familiar. Jargon is confusing to outsiders, which is why you should avoid using it for general audiences. But for tribes, it can be a sign of connection. "One word which we use a lot here," an assistant treasurer told me, "which I don't think even exists, is *monetize.*" Which means? "Sell. We monetized an asset. We converted it to cash. We sold it. But we use the word monetize. And I don't even know why we do that. Maybe it sounds more highfalutin. It makes it sound harder than it really was, so you get extra credit for having accomplished it." What he is pointing out is the dual purposes of jargon: first, jargon draws a line between groups, which means if you can use a group's jargon well, it's more likely people will think you know what you're talking about. And second, jargon has a built-in spin; it presents a perceptual viewpoint.

When you know how and why jargon is used, you can use it more effectively to spin your message for the audience you're addressing. Usually, you'll want to ally yourself with your audience, and, in that case, you should learn their jargon and use it, both in speaking and in writing. But sometimes you will want to reinforce the perception that you are from a different tribe; perhaps one with expertise your audience doesn't share. A touch of jargon here and there can signal them that there is a body of knowledge that you're familiar with and that they might want to rely on your expertise.

Verbal Style. Not only do tribes create their own dialects, but they have their own accents, idioms, inflections, and tempos. I once had a boss from South Carolina who possessed not only a wonderful drawl but a verbal delivery that recalled muggy Southern days when just moving your tongue seems to require great effort. Tom wasn't slow-witted—he just spoke slowly and precisely, while his ideas percolated. A friend of mine who was raised in New Jersey and now lives in Italy gets to her point with a rapid-fire barrage of language. They're both effective—but they don't mix.

You don't need to try to match your audience's accent—that's an obvious contrivance—but it's important to match their pace. A speed mismatch is a red flag that you're not of their world ("I don't trust that fast-talking guy," or "She was so California-mellow it was frustrating.")

Organizations have styles as well. At the California Credit Union League, Dan Niebrugge, the director of member services, characterized the conversations there as open and without guile. It's a style that's fitting with that grassroots, service-oriented institution. The talk in the hallways of the Los Angeles County Bar Association, on the other hand, is quick and witty; the kind of bantering and verbal pirouettes you would expect lawyers to enjoy. If you were to use either style among the other crowd, you'd quickly be marked as an outsider—someone to be wary of.

Nonverbal Cues. The way people use their body to deliver messages is yet another communication channel that is often tribe-specific. People in deadline-driven industries such as advertising or journalism may tend to have impatient mannerisms compared with bankers, for example. In other fields, there's the broadly gesturing salesperson, the constrained director of computing, or the professorial air of the researcher. In each case, these people can recognize and relate to their own. If you want to reach them, notice and match (or at least don't conflict with) their nonverbal style.

And don't neglect your chances to reinforce the bonds within your tribe by using nonverbal cues. Tom Harrison explains:

> You can just say, "I got a phone call from Bill," and roll your eyes. They know everything. Your coworker knows exactly what that means. And that's normal. And we need to remember to do that with superiors and with clients as well, where we take advantage of what we've experienced together and point to it regularly. It says, "We have tribal stories together."

Anything at All. People usually want to feel a connection, want to discover more members of their own tribe, and want to feel good about that tribe. It's why when we talk about the weather, we agree that it's been just too darn hot and that we're the type of people who don't like it when it's too darn hot. This kind of conversation serves as an orienting preamble and isn't something to avoid. It may seem like a stall until the real communication begins (something I warned about earlier), yet as long as there is real interest from your audience in making this initial connection, you should follow it for as far as seems wise. Then switch to your pitch.

It's Your Message—But Should It Come From You?

Sometimes tribal lines can be tricky—you might not always be able to put yourself in the in-group. I once proposed a project to my boss, who told me there was a good chance that the president of the company would approve it. She didn't, however, tell me *she* would pitch the idea to him. Instead, she told me she'd help me draft a memo, which would be sent to *her*.

My boss realized that to be effective, this message had to come from a particular tribe and be delivered to a particular tribe. If she had gone to the president directly, that would have reinforced her link to her own department, which made it more likely that the president would see her as "from the outside." Yet the message couldn't go from me to the president, bypassing my boss as the head of her own department. Her solution was to draw the lines in such a way that she, as vice president, and the president would evaluate my proposal as members of the same tribe—senior management—even though she'd helped formulate the message.

While getting on the right side of the *us* vs. *them* equation will give you an edge in your communication, that alone won't keep your audience listening or reading. To do that, you have to convince them that you're worth listening to, which we cover next.

15

Boost Your Authority

As Aristotle noted, people judge information by who offers it. If you're respected, your information will be respected—a heuristic known as the influence of *authority*.

Among heuristics, authority is a monster. Research has shown that people will even commit cruel acts if they have confidence in the authority of the message-giver. In the 1970s, Yale psychology professor Stanley Milgram set up an experiment in which subjects were instructed by a "researcher" in a lab coat to give excruciating electric shocks to people when they gave wrong answers to a quiz and not to stop no matter how much the people screamed or begged, which they did. The shocks weren't real; the "victims" were actors faking pain. Before Milgram began his experiments, psychology students predicted one in a hundred would keep up the shocks; a group of psychiatrists predicted one in a thousand. The results? *Two thirds* of the people were willing to follow the authority figure's orders.

Despite its scary overtones, we all depend on authority to some degree; otherwise, society would come unglued. Because the working world is a maze of hierarchies and competing tribes, virtually every message must have some authority spin, or it will be cast aside.

Consider, for example, phoning someone you don't know. If you're making a cold call to Warren Buffet and you reach his receptionist, you'll probably be asked to leave a message. But if you're returning his call, that signals the receptionist that your message has been authorized by Mr. Buffet himself and is cleared to be received. If you know him personally, you might say, "Is Warren there?" indicating that you're a close friend and that you've got the authority to speak to him. These messages get through because they've been authorized to precede or preempt other competing messages.

When you need to create a compelling argument, authority becomes even more important. Facts must be justified, sources cited, and opinions backed up. To craft an effective authority spin, you need to understand what creates authority in the first place. Authority is made up of any one or a combination of three ingredients:

Power. In hierarchies, some people have more power than others; those with power can make both pleasant and unpleasant things happen, which is why we all pay attention to what the boss says. Although this kind of authority is usually exercised up and down the chain of command inside a company, some people or agencies outside can also get messages through by the sheer force of their power. For example, when the IRS calls—about anything—people listen.

Expertise. By far the most common, and sensible, use of authority is authority that's grounded in knowledge, training, or experience. Because of its value, we've worked out an intricate system of signals that help indicate expertise. Advanced college degrees, seniority systems, professional licensing, and membership in professional groups exist to validate expertise. Other ways of demonstrating expertise include long years of experience, teaching, writing a book or article, or serving as a consultant.

Status. Status is the shadow world of expertise. People, institutions, or facts may have status because of their fame and reputation, which may or may not correlate with the amount of credibility they have. All other things being equal, most of us would value the word of a professor from Harvard over one from Podunk University. Status can also exert a force clearly outside the bounds of expertise, as when a famous actor tells us how great his new Chevrolet is.

Any combination of these three components can be present in a single source of authority. Companies such as Microsoft or people such as *New Yorker* editor Tina Brown have all three.

Who Are You?

Naturally, the starting point for the authority in your message is you. We all realize people must know something about us before they'll accept our word, yet we also know that no one trusts a braggart. Most of us solve this dilemma by picking a comfortable level of self-advertising and sticking with it in all situations. But the key to adding the right amount of spin to your message is to judge how much your audience needs to know about your authority. Offer too little, and you won't be taken seriously. Offer too much, and people will take it as a sign that there's a hollowness behind your bravado.

In conversations, you can add bits of authority spin as you go along, monitoring your audience's understanding and adjusting as needed. If they don't seem to be acknowledging that you know what you're talking about, you add information. One classic authority spin is name dropping—a technique that, despite its bad reputation, works well if you can do it subtly. Remember that the name doesn't have to be that of a person; it can be a company, institution, piece of software that you know, book that you've read, or any other name you can associate yourself with that adds to your power, expertise, or status. One technique is to bring the name into the conversation gradually by introducing it in an anonymous fashion and then revealing it. You might begin by saying, "A friend of mine who knows about this told me . . ." and then later reveal that your friend is Connie Chung. If you're lucky, your audience will ask who it is before you have to slip it in.

Below are examples of phrases that can be added to conversations. I've arranged them according to the three categories of authority and in increasing degrees of chutzpah:

Power

"Someone on my staff will . . ."

"As director of marketing at my company, I run across this kind of thing a lot."

"I try to run my company according to certain precepts . . ."

"I'll have Senator Dole get back to you on that."

Expertise

"I've done some reading in this area, and one theory used
is . . ."

"During my five years at Beebop Entertainment, we dealt
with this a lot."

"A colleague of mine has done a study that says . . ."

"As an attorney, I deal with this situation often."

"I wrote an article on this subject, and my premise was . . ."

"In my book I tried to show that . . ."

"Steven Hawking called me with that question just the other
day."

Status

"The *Business Journal* seemed to like the way I handled that
situation."

"I've been misquoted in the media, so you might think I . . ."

"I hope Barbara Walters doesn't ask me that when I go on her
show next week."

If you're giving a presentation or a speech, you should
establish your authority at the beginning, so that your ensuing
argument benefits from the full weight of your authority.

If you're giving a formal speech, chances are you'll be
introduced. If you can write your own introduction, you can make
sure it includes everything your audience needs to know about your
power, expertise, or authority—and that should be a lot. Remember
that since the words won't be coming out of your mouth, your
credentials will seem more valid and less like bragging. If you can't
write your own introduction, listen carefully to the one you're given
for any gaps in your authority. If your titles are listed, but not your

accomplishments, take note—titles can mean nothing to an audience unless they know the significance of them. If your status in your field isn't revealed, note that too. As soon as you begin your speech, your job will be to fill in the blanks so your audience will have a good idea of what your opinion means.

If you're subjected to a bad introduction, you'll have to work fast to counter it, or everything you say will be tainted. I was once interviewed on a radio program about a business book I wrote. I was stunned when the interviewer introduced me with a random line from my biography—that I'd played guitar in a rock band—and left it at that. The radio audience was left wondering what in the world this rock and roller could possibly say about business. I knew that the first thing I had to say—no matter what question she asked me—was that *after* my rock and roll days I spent more than twenty years as a professional in corporate communications and had written three books on the subject.

Even if your introduction is good, you may need to remind your audience of your authority by referring to your experience as you go along. Reminding your audience of how you solved that tough problem for Viacom and how that applies to the subject at hand will keep your authority fresh.

It's even more important to announce your authority when you'll get little or no introduction, as often happens when you're giving a presentation inside your company. You may be introduced simply as "Sheila from accounting, who's here to explain the new purchasing system."

In these cases, you must begin by highlighting your power, expertise, and/or status yourself. The less well-known you are to the audience, the more formally you should present your background. Here's an example:

Hello, I'm Frank Meyers, and today I'll be presenting our marketing plan for JavaLove coffee. As assistant brand manager, I'm responsible for media planning and public relations efforts for all our company's coffee products. My education and background are in advertising, and I worked on the agency side before Bill Fern hired me to come here to Bigtime Food Products.

In other situations, you might be well-known, but your background might not be. Then you'll need to take a more casual approach, something like:

I'll be filling you in on our marketing plan for JavaLove coffee. Now the media and public relations plan I've cooked up is a little different from the other brands I manage. I'll be using a technique I learned when I worked at Wellington Advertising, just before I moved over here.

The trick is to communicate the same information in a way that doesn't sound like you're bragging.

In written communication, establishing your credentials depends on the form. E-mail and letters tend to be similar to conversations, so allusions to your authority can be woven in just as you might if you were talking face to face. Because formal reports are usually written in the third person, it's harder to squeeze in your expertise. Sometimes you can use passive phrases such as "experience at Swerdlow industries has shown," which is effective if your reader knows that you were the one at Swerdlow. Sometimes it's appropriate to include a biography of yourself at the end of a report—some Requests for Proposals require one of each person who will be working on the proposed project.

Too Much of a Good Thing

Authority is powerful and not always good; too much can sometimes get in the way of communication. The director of the school my daughter attended would occasionally call me at my office, and when she did, the first thing she would make clear was that the call was not about a problem with Jordan. She had learned from too many panicky parents that the authority of her name, whether on the phone or on a message, would instantly spook her audience into thinking their child was injured. After that, they couldn't hear anything else. The same syndrome occurs with the boss who appears only when it's time to issue orders or edicts. On the day when she really needs free-flowing, uninhibited suggestions, her staff will be too nervous to come up with any.

It's natural to look for ways to increase the authority of your messages when they're headed up the chain, but it's important to make sure the messages going down aren't carrying too much. If you need information from people in lower positions, especially if they also work in your general area of knowledge, make clear your ignorance. Phrases such as "I know the theory, but I really don't know how we do it here" or "I'm pretty rusty on this stuff" will reap more rewards than the usual "give me a report on our activities."

Call In the Experts

Besides establishing your own authority, you must establish the authority of your material. When done right, there's a strange phenomenon that occurs. Your argument won't seem to be an argument at all. The illusion you create is that the facts lead inescapably to a single conclusion.

Working to improve the authoritative spin of your message is different from researching facts to support your argument, although each has an influence on the other. You can gather all the amazing facts you want, but if your audience isn't convinced that they come from reliable sources, the facts won't do you any good. Conversely, you might run across impressive authorities who say things that *almost* support your thesis. Choosing facts with just the right combination of relevancy and authority is the trick.

Obviously, if you have impressive resources, you'll cite them, but you should do more than that to get the most impact. How you do it depends on how much your audience knows about the source.

Authority Your Audience Knows. Just because you think your audience knows your source or you think a person's title or an institution's name declares their authority, you shouldn't stop there. You'll increase the spin if you add at least a short, qualifying phrase that highlights the power, expertise, or status of the source. Here are some samples:

Power

Director of Urban Planning John C. Talbot, who heads the statewide board controlling parking regulations

The South Coast Air Quality Management District, the regulating agency for southern California

The Chicago Manual of Style, the standard reference for the publishing industry

Expertise

Dr. John C. Talbot, Professor of Business, Sierra Madre University, an acknowledged expert in the field

John C. Talbot, author of *The Extruded Plastics Sourcebook*

Nobel laureate John C. Talbot

Status

John C. Talbot, lead investigator in the "Son of Sam" homicide case

Harvard professor John C. Talbot

Best-selling author John C. Talbot

By adding a short phrase you'll remind people that they should be impressed and will orient anyone who doesn't know your source. The only time to avoid this is if by doing so you'll insult the intelligence of your audience. In group settings or reports, that's unlikely; people who know your source will assume you're qualifying it for the benefit of others who don't know. In one-on-one conversations you can gauge your listener's reaction, adding more if he or she doesn't seem sufficiently impressed. In letters, memos, or e-mail directed to a single person, you'll have to take your best guess, although it's always better to say too much than too little.

Authority Your Audience Doesn't Know. If you know your audience isn't familiar with your sources, your job of emphasizing authority is tougher, but it's also a greater opportunity. If they have no independent judgment of your source, they have to rely on your characterization of it. In that case, you have to add more spin. For example, you might say, "Dr. John C. Talbot, Professor of Business at Sierra Madre University, has been a leading management theorist for more than twenty years and has conducted eighteen studies on employee relations. His recommendations have been adopted by several Fortune 500 companies, including Chrysler Corporation." All this may be a necessary preface to a single fact or quote from Dr. Talbot. Your goal is to hit as many of the three kinds of authority—power, expertise, and status—as possible. In this example, expertise is implied by Talbot's title, years of work, and number of studies conducted. Power is implied by stating that he's influenced the decisions of major companies, and status by naming a well-known corporation.

Implied Authority. Just as it's important to know when, and how much, to qualify your sources, it's important to know when not to. There are two general cases when this is true: when the fact you're introducing is common knowledge and when the fact can't be qualified without a long-winded technical orientation. Here you'll just have to state your fact and move on.

What's crucial is that your fact sounds like a fact and not an opinion; that is, that what you're saying can be verified. For example, you might say, "Because camping equipment sales peak in April, the rollout of our new Wondertent should be in March." Unless there's a clear reason not to believe you, your audience will generally accept the first part of that statement—"camping equipment sales peak in April"—as a fact, because the alternative is to assume that you just made it up. Unless you have no credibility at all, most people will believe you.

The Oblique Endorsement. If you need to boost the authority of your message but can't find a source that speaks directly about your subject, don't give up. Instead of citing a fact, link your opinion to the opinion of someone with authority.

You might, for example, mention the general view of an influential coworker or manager in a preface to your point. "I share Sarah's concern that profits will erode if we don't support our dealers," you might say, and then, "which is why our new promotion will be so important.'"

You can also imply authority by including your team, department, or company in your statement. "We've studied this problem thoroughly," you may begin, "and I think there is a solution."

In some cases, it may be appropriate to imply authority by mentioning professors you have studied with or well-known consultants you learned from. Discussing their expertise just before you offer your opinion implies that your thinking is an extension of theirs.

You can also cite the opinions of experts with whom you have no connection. For example, if your argument rests on your belief that your company will become more and more reliant on the accurate gathering of information, you might use a quote from a futurist such as Alvin Toffler that states that *all* businesses will become more information dependent. If your idea continues in the same vein, Toffler's reputation will help boost your credibility.

17

Give In to Win

The marketing representatives was restless. The company hadn't been faring well against the competition, and now the marketing director was about to appear to give them a pep talk. What would he say? Would he claim that sales weren't as bad as they looked? Would he say that their competitors' successes were short-term or figments of their paranoid imagination? Would he urge them to pull together, try a little harder, buck up and stop complaining? They sat there, arms crossed, waiting.

The marketing director said none of these things. He stood up, and instead of taking cover behind a podium, he sat casually on the edge of a desk. And then he told the reps why their fears about their company were *true*. He knew a secret about spin: If you give in on one point, you can often win all the others.

One who was there remembers how he did it. "He spoke very frankly about our weaknesses. He was saying, here's what we don't do as well as the competitor. We're not as good as them at working with people further down the supply chain to pull through sales. We're not as good at that. *And we're probably not going to try to become as good at that.*"

Immediately, the crowd's attitude changed from suspicion to acceptance. "People felt like, 'Wow, he's telling me the real stuff.' " His demeanor added to the effect:

He did all this sitting down, and without notes. And yet it wasn't rambling. I've seen that done before, sitting down without notes, the Jimmy Carter put-on-the-cardigan kind of thing, but they ramble and you begin to think, "come on, give me a break here." I almost get the idea that he practiced it. And that part of the triumph of it was that he could make it sound like he was doing it extemporaneously.

It was an excellent use of the *Give In to Win* spin. Before his audience had even had a chance to pose their argument, he agreed with them. They were all on the same side.

From there, he moved on to the points that would have been impossible for his audience to hear if he hadn't diffused their worry. He said, here are our strengths, and here's what we can do.

The force that makes this spin work is a variation of the reciprocity principle called *reciprocal concessions*. As I pointed out earlier, we humans are exquisitely sensitive to the give-and-take relationships we have with each other. Favors are to be repaid with favors. In an argument, one of the most powerful favors you can offer the other side is to concede that they're right about something.

As soon as you do, you trigger feelings of reciprocity: they'll then feel like they owe a concession to you.

Like the general reciprocity rule, it's the exchange that matters more than the actual value or nature of each concession. If you admit that the other side's *ideas* are correct, they might admit that your *plan for action* is right. Christopher Matthews, in his book *Hardball*, advises "Always concede on principle," something he shows is a favorite tact of politicians. "When sitting down to a deal," he says, "they always separate the principle at stake from the actual stakes. Then, with the air thick with melodrama, they concede on the principle—and rake in the chips."

That's exactly what the savvy marketing director did. He admitted that the reps had the right idea—that their company was just plain worse than their competitors in some areas. In exchange, he got their commitment to do better.

When you can't swap principles for stakes, you can trade larger requests for smaller ones, in what psychology professor Robert Cialdini calls the "rejection-then-retreat" technique. It's a spin that we're all familiar with: Ask for something big, then when you're rejected, ask for something smaller. What you might not know is how powerful the effect is.

Professor Cialdini wanted to find out, so he and his associates conducted an experiment. In the first phase of the experiment, they asked random college students to participate in their "County Youth Counseling Program" by volunteering to take a group of wayward kids to the zoo for a day. Fewer than twenty percent said they would. In the second phase, they approached students and first asked if they'd spent two hours a week for two years counseling troubled kids. Naturally, they were turned down flat by all the students. But they followed this up with the same request they'd made in phase one—to take these kids to the zoo for just a day. This time, softened up by the first question, half the students said yes.

Besides the reciprocity, this style of *Give In to Win* spin works because of the effect of contrast. Compared to a big initial request, a reduced request seems much smaller.

This doesn't automatically mean that the more you ask for, the more you'll eventually get. Another study has shown that if your first request is clearly outrageous, then your concession will be seen as fake and won't work. The overriding rule of giving in to win is that it must be clear to your audience that, at first, you're genuinely working against your own self-interest. Later, it seems only fair that you should get something for your willingness to compromise.

Get a Commitment

We humans hate to be inconsistent, and we'll avoid that feeling if at all possible. Psychologists call it our dislike of *cognitive dissonance*, which is the state of having to believe two conflicting ideas at the same time. That means that if you can show somebody that what you're saying is part of what they're already committed to, then they'll agree with you so they don't have to disagree with themselves. In other words, if Frank believes he's good at cutting fat from a budget and you convince him that what you're suggesting he cut *is* fat, then he must agree with you and cut it.

By studying your audience, as I've suggested earlier, you should have some clues about what's important to your target that might match up with parts of your message. You can then use phrases such as "You've always been a strong proponent of employee education" or "This is an extension of your results-oriented program" to link your idea with their convictions.

If your message doesn't seem to connect with any of your audience's beliefs or if you don't know anything about your audience, commitment spin will still work. To use it, you begin by getting a small commitment from your target, which you can spin into a larger commitment.

The effect has been demonstrated in many social psychology experiments. My favorite is one in which researchers asked people to display a 3-inch-square sign to support safe driving. Naturally, most people thought that was a good cause, and nearly all agreed. Next, the researchers asked that group and a new group if they would be willing to have a gigantic (and ugly) billboard placed in their front yard that said "Drive Carefully." Of the new group, only 17 percent agreed. But the group that had first agreed to display the small sign reacted differently. They didn't want to look like hypocrites, so 76 percent agreed.

Growing Legs

One of the reasons the first group was more agreeable is that they'd been given time for their commitment to "grow legs." What happens is this: When we commit ourselves to a new idea, it becomes integrated into our constellation of beliefs. It forms positive links to ideas we already have, and new ideas are formed that support it. We convince ourselves that we did the right thing. The idea grows legs.

Although you can sometimes move your audience from a small commitment to a larger one in a single communication, adding the right amount of time *between* communication gives your target time to grow legs on the idea. Spacing your communication out in a series of messages also lets you make adjustments based on what your audience is doing. Trying to do too much in one message can be unpredictable.

Another aspect of consistency is this: Once we start working toward an agreement, we develop a commitment to seeing it through. Otherwise, it seems we've wasted our time. It's why people hate to pull out of deals, and it's why starting and continuing interaction is essential to commitment spin. Using phrases such as "We're so close to a deal, let's not backtrack now" can help put this spin into action.

Other Eyes

People are especially concerned about their consistency as seen by others, which means that in general, resolve strengthens when we're in a group situation. If you know this, you can set your spin accordingly.

If you're certain that you'll get agreement, try to get it in the presence of others. If you're in a group situation and you run into resistance, back off. Fighting will only strengthen your opponents' commitment to their side. "You never become confrontational in any group setting," says marketing consultant Jan Baird, "because I think it builds up a wall that becomes even more difficult to tear down. You stand firm, state your point of view, but you don't attack the person."

Is It Real?

The trapdoor of commitment spin is when you succeed in winning the argument but still lose your audience. For commitment to motivate people, it must be true agreement. The mistake too many people make is to argue until the other side acquiesces and says anything it can to get rid of you. Jan makes sure she understands what's going on inside the head and heart of her target. "If they walk away," she says, "and you've simply overcome their objections but you haven't really changed their heart, their mindset, you haven't accomplished anything. So yes, you can walk away feeling glib and say 'Oh, yeah, I got them,' but you didn't. You didn't get what you came for if you just won the conversation."

Compared to What?

One day more than twenty years ago my wife and her friend were sitting at home when a man selling vacuum cleaners came to the door. After he'd finished his impressive demonstration, he told the two women what they were waiting to hear: the price. "This machine," he said, "is priced at less than $400." They were ready to ask him to pack up and take his overpriced rug-sucker with him, when he added, "In fact, its price is only $189." They both bought one. I'm happy to report ours still functions perfectly.

That salesman was taking advantage of a phenomenon known as *perceptual contrast*. It means that we perceive things as bigger or smaller, longer or shorter, depending on what that thing is compared with. In this case, the lesser price seemed like pocket change after the teeth-rattling sum of $400.

Like many kinds of spin, spin based on perceptual contrast can control you if you don't control it. If you don't know what someone is using to compare your price, specifications, delivery time, or number of meetings, you can't know how out of whack your message might sound. Putting quantities in perspective with comments such as "This shouldn't take anywhere near the six months these projects usually take" will make your estimate of three months seem like a blink instead of eternity.

A variation of this spin is to purposefully emphasize the chance that you will utterly and completely fail at your project. You might say, for example, "I don't see how we could possibly meet the sales goal, but we'll give it our best shot." Any success you have will then seem like a tremendous victory. In cases where you can't in good conscience say you'll fail, you can spin expectations by building a cushion into your estimates. When you deliver way ahead of time and far under budget, your accomplishment will seem all the greater.

Spin on the Phone

Making a phone call isn't the single channel of communication it used to be. Now it's a wheel of chance where you might talk to the person you want, talk to a person who'll pass a message to the person you want, or leave a recording for the person you want via voice mail. A single phone call offers several ways to spin. Let's take them one at a time.

The Person You Want. When you're talking live to someone you can use much of the spin you'd use if you were having a face-to-face conversation, although you can improve a spin's effect with a little preparation.

You can increase authoritative spin over the phone by reeling off facts, statistics, anecdotes, or point-by-point arguments seemingly off-the-cuff, when actually they're written and in front of you. To make this effective, don't write yourself a script. Most of your notes should be bullet points—simple reminders that will force you to use your own words. Avoid writing full sentences, or you'll find yourself reading them and sounding stilted.

Speaking close to the phone and in a hushed voice will emphasize the secrecy (and therefore the value) of what you're saying.

Telling someone that you're taking notes reminds the person of commitment, which can be a compliment (your ideas are so good I want to get them down) or a gentle warning (you'll be held to what you say here).

The Message-Taker. If you're talking to a receptionist or anyone who's going to take a message for the person you're trying to reach, realize that you've now got two audiences: the message-taker and your final target. Message-takers aren't recording devices. They'll add their own spin to a message depending at least partly on the spin you've delivered it with. Make sure to acknowledge the message-taker as a separate audience. Speak to him or her directly instead of launching into "tell Richard that the Fielding account . . ."

You can improve your chances of good communication by using the "Make It Their Idea" hook. Ask the message-taker for his or her opinion: Should you leave a message or call back later? If the answer is call back later, ask when might be the best time to call. This interaction helps make you and the message-taker partners in trying to reach your target. If you're advised to call back at a certain time yet you'd really rather leave a message, don't rebuff the message-taker by refusing the advice—just agree to call back later. Then, in ten minutes or so, call back and explain that your schedule has changed and you won't be able to call back at that time—you'll have to leave a message. This extended interchange reinforces the idea of you and the message-taker as a team.

For most receptionists, their job is to record messages as accurately as possible. Yet they have another function, especially in smaller offices; that is, to act as a filter. Part of their job is to try and sort out the messages with the bigger authority flags and pass them on first. If you've got one of those flags—you're a friend, you're returning your target's call, you've been hired by your target and need information, or whatever—don't forget to wave it. If you can't claim this kind of authority, there are a few other spins that can help.

One is urgency. Asking that you be called back by a certain time, or between certain hours, can imply importance. Another is to leave a message that uses the "It's New" hook, simply by saying that you have some news you need to tell your target. A third is to pique curiosity—"The Lure of the Unavailable"—by leaving just enough information to create some interest. These can't be empty promises; when you do speak to your target, you'd better deliver, or communication will shut down.

Voice Mail. If you think of voice mail as the audio version of those little message pads that say so-and-so-called, you're missing the full range of communication in this relatively new medium. Voice-mail presents several variables you should consider and control to influence your spin. They are the message itself, the emotional tone, the background sound, and the time you call.

The message. Unlike leaving a message with a message-taker, who can ask questions such as "And you're with?" or "Will Mr. Kissenger know what this is regarding?" voice mail gives you complete control over the information you include or exclude. Yet most people don't see this as the powerful communication opportunity it is. Instead, they'll choose between only two types of messages: the "my message is too complicated—I'll just ask her to call me back" message or the "I just have a quick question, so I'll leave it on his voice mail" message.

"Quick question" messages are often appropriate and efficient. But when you've got a lot to discuss, don't take the lazy way out and say, "Jim, it's Bob. Call me." Consider all of the information you could leave, then pick portions of it that will create a hook or a spin. Think of voice mail as your private broadcasting station and your message as a teaser that invites your listener to tune in to another program (you) later on. Just as TV spots don't say, "Please watch the news at eleven" but instead say, "Aliens land in Cucamonga! Film at eleven!" you should cull from your information that which is most enticing.

You might create an "It's New" hook by saying, "I was going over some figures and I think I found a major problem." Or you can add authority spin by mentioning a name: "Bill Bates suggested I call you." You can create *Give In to Win* spin by saying, "I've thought about your objections to the plan, and I think you're right. Let's go over the details."

You can offer a "Make It Their Idea" hook. "I was looking through my Rolodex," you might say, "and I realized that the last time I talked to you, you were about to launch a new product line. I thought I'd give you a call and see how that worked out." Most people like to talk about themselves, and this hook provides that opportunity.

Emotional tone. Your voice carries much more information than what's in your words. You can sound depressed, energetic, harried, enthusiastic, frustrated, or stern, and unless you're paying attention, you can unconsciously put the wrong spin on your message no matter what the words say—especially if you're aggravated after having just listened to an irritating message someone left on *your* voice mail. "Voice mail is the most dangerous kind of communication there is," one executive told me. "The problem with voice mail is you can be trapped. It's a siren song. Somebody says something, and you hear their voice, voices convey emotion, both good and bad, and you respond to emotion."

If you prepare, you can use a measured amount of emotion to spin innocuous words into a very pointed message. For example, you can say, "I left a message before, but you must have been too busy to return it" in a tone either filled with understanding or dripping with sarcasm. The phrase, "Could you stay late and finish up the Somerset report?" can be expressed as a question or a command, depending on tone.

Make sure you know the message and the emotional tone you're going to use for your message before you dial, otherwise it's easy to get caught up short and blurt out something that you'll later have to explain "didn't come out the way I meant it to."

Background sound. I'm always amazed at the amount of extraneous sound a phone will pick up. As I was talking to my editor one day, she asked about some music she could hear in the background. "Is that an ice-cream truck going by?" she asked. It was. She could hear it on the street even though I was calling from my office on the second floor in the back of my house.

Background sound can tell a listener a number of things: that you're calling from a cubicle and don't have your own office; that you're calling from a phone booth; that others are in your office and everybody's waiting for a decision.

If you call the office from a trade convention, and there's a party going on in the background (as there often seems to be at some conventions), it might not connote that you're hard at work. If you're late for an appointment and have a cellular phone, you might want to call from your car instead of the office to show you're on your way.

Time you called. Most voice mail has a time stamp, and that small piece of information can speak volumes. If you call your boss at 3:00 p.m. and leave a message that you're on your way home and will check with her tomorrow, she might wonder why you're not staying until five. Savvy voice mailers might leave at three but call the boss's message line at six-thirty, leaving a long message about work. You don't have to say *where* you're calling from (remember background noise here), and even if it's clear that you're calling from home, it's impressive that you're still dealing with work-related issues into the evening.

To sum up, voice mail shouldn't be ad-libbed but should be composed just as a letter or memo would be. Consider all four components here: the amount of information, your emotional tone, the background sound, and the time you call. For casual messages, it only takes a moment to run through this as a mental checklist before leaving a message. For more important communications, you may want to write it down or record a test message to see that all your components are in place.

A sidelight of interest here is that voice mail is not as private as you might think. In a court case that has yet to be decided, one man is suing his former employer who had recorded the man's voice mail messages sent to his lover. The employer then played the recordings to the man's wife. When the man confronted his boss about it, he was fired. The clash between an employee's right to privacy and a company's right to have their phones used for business will probably be protracted. In the meantime, it's wise not to leave anything on voice mail that might come back to haunt you.

Gauging the Tip-Off Factor. The effectiveness of spin depends on the initial state of mind of your audience, which can be changed not just by your communication, but by your *attempts* to communicate. Someone who's been alerted that you're trying to reach them will have a different reaction to your message than someone who hasn't. Social service agency director Pat Bowie changes her strategy depending on her target and message:

A lot of times—and I think I do this unconsciously—I will have something I really have to discuss with someone and I'll call and I will get voice mail; I won't leave a message, because I want to get that person cold. I don't want them to know what I'm calling about, or that I'm calling. I want to get *them*.

There will be other times when I want the person to know that I'm calling and even give them an idea on the phone of what I'm calling about so that they aren't caught off-guard. And a lot of times it will depend on who the person is. If I have never interacted with a person yet it's a real important issue, most of the time I won't leave a message. I'll call back until I get them. Because first impressions are always so important.

Give and Take—Again. The last thing to remember about phone calls is that they're subject to the rules of reciprocity, just like any other interaction. If Marco has called you several times and you haven't returned his calls, then you're on the negative side of his balance sheet. That leaves you open to being guilted by him the next time he calls. On the other hand, if you've stacked up a number of voice mail messages (which you can do intentionally by calling when you know someone's out) without getting a call back, then you've got a little extra leverage.

When it's time for your ideas to move from conversation to commitment to paper, new opportunities for spin open up—based on the way we *see* what we read. It's the visual spin of the written word we'll look at next.

Spin on Paper

In an earlier chapter, I talked about the first impression—the hook—that a document's form can trigger. In this chapter, we'll delve into the interior of documents to see how visual style can create spin.

Before the rise of personal computers, there wasn't much visual spin you could put on day-to-day business communication on paper without spending a lot of money for typesetting and printing. With word processors and desktop publishing, that's all changed. Visual standards are now much higher. In fact, the way a report, proposal, letter, or even a memo looks can make the difference between convincing your audience and losing them. Jack Montgomery recalls a time when his company lost clients because they had fallen behind:

Our competitor was ahead of us in all these computer analyses we would do on structure and design reviews. We would do things that were more "back of the envelope" but we'd come to the same—or, I think, better, more technically enlightened—conclusions. But they would come in with something that had been printed on a color computer printer, with a lot of different colors involved in the time and temperature plot, or whatever else—often stupid things, once you saw what it was they were getting across—but they looked great. They had found a spin that captured the customer's imagination.

Eventually, everyone in Jack's field got the same kind of computers, and the playing field was level.

What Jack experienced has to do with the fact that people are less anxious to shoot down something that seems to carry prestige or status in the first place. Two researchers found this out when they arranged an experiment to see who would get honked at by angry drivers first: someone in a new luxury car or someone in a heap. In both cases, the drivers just sat in front of a green light. Almost everyone behind the junker honked twice or more; two of them just rammed into the car's bumper. More than half of those behind the impressive auto never touched their horns at all.

Documents have prestige and status, too, based on the way they look. For hundreds of years we've been conditioned to think that something set in type and printed is "truer" than something typewritten. This used to have some validity to it: anybody could get their hands on a typewriter, but a typeset document implied that a publisher, editor, and perhaps even a researcher had checked the information and deemed it worthy of being printed. Now, of course, anyone with a decent word processor can produce something that looks printed. Yet our associations linger. It's a not-too-distant cousin to the heuristic of authority. Type has an authoritative spin that typewriting doesn't.

Unfortunately, many people armed with word processors go wild, using fonts and layouts that are far from professional-looking, thereby destroying their authoritative impact. To avoid this, you need only learn a few basic principles of publication design.

Use the Right Font. Like clothing, fonts can connote dependability or flakiness, conservatism or decadence. Just as you wouldn't want your business attire to distract people from you, the fonts you choose shouldn't distract people from your message.

Although you can spend a lifetime studying fonts, you don't need to if you only want to use fonts with the most authoritative spin in standard documents such as memos, reports, and letters. (Advertising is something else and should be left to experts.) For text, use Times Roman and its italic, bold, and bold italic variations. For headlines, use Helvetica and its italic, bold, extra bold, bold italic, or condensed variations.

Times Roman is the single most popular English typeface in the world. It is used for hundreds of thousands of publications, and for that reason, there is virtually no chance that it will distract your reader. Because it's so familiar, it immediately calls up subtle associations with authoritative books and magazines. If you use it in all your documents, you will gain the maximum typographic authority with a minimum of risk.

Helvetica is nearly as popular for headlines as Times Roman is for text and has the same authoritative connotations. The only acceptable exception to this scheme is to use Times Roman for both your text and your headline, which is fine if you don't want to go to the trouble of switching fonts. As popular as Helvetica is (and even though it is often used for text) you should never use it for the text of your business documents—it can be hard to read and tends to look cold.

Use Font Variations Correctly. Even if you stick to the fonts I recommend above, you can ruin the effect if you misuse the bold, italic, or uppercase variations. Since publishers never produce books and magazines that are printed with all bold, all italic, or all uppercase lettering, neither should you—these variations are hard to read and are a dead giveaway that you're an amateur. If you want to emphasize a word or phrase, italicize it or use bold, not all caps. Headlines should also be in lowercase, although each word can begin with a capital letter (in the style of many newspapers) if that seems appropriate.

Make Your Text Easy to Skim. Since the chances are excellent that someone will skim your document before reading it, don't fight against your reader by presenting a large, undivided mass of text. Reports, letters, and even memos should be divided into shorter sections, each topped with a bold subhead that is in itself a mini-hook. Even when this isn't appropriate (for example, in a short *mea culpa* business letter), good writers give a lot of thought to the first and last sentences in a paragraph, because these are the ones a reader sees when skimming.

Do not use an outline form with several indentations as a layout style. It wastes paper (making your document take more pages, which makes it more daunting) and can produce narrow columns that are hard to read. The effect of an outline can be achieved by first creating a document with an internal hierarchy; you can then show that hierarchy by dividing it into appropriate sections: chapters, subsections with subheads, or paragraphs that begin with a sentence set in bold.

Use Size. Psychological studies have shown that size and status are related. In one experiment, college students were given cards that announced the amount of money they'd win or have to pay, up to plus or minus three dollars. Although the cards were all the same size, the students remembered the larger amounts, whether positive or negative, as being on bigger cards.

Since we associate importance and size, you can make something in a document seem more important by increasing its size. For example, if a company has three strong, old divisions and one new, weak one, the wimpy division can seem stronger if its section in a report is just as big and bold as the others. In a long report, you can increase the size of the headline for each section. Headlines in business documents, though, should still be conservatively sized so you don't create a screaming tabloid effect: Headlines should never be more than three times the size of the text type.

Spin on E-Mail

One of the fundamental points of this book is that as communication channels become more crowded, we must become better at attracting attention to our messages. While nearly everyone admits this is true, few people realize how fast communication channels are clogging. E-mail was supposed to help us communicate so easily and efficiently that even people impossible to reach on the phone would respond to a short, friendly e-mail. It's been said that Bill Gates reads every e-mail message he gets. According to the *Los Angeles Times*, Bill gets 3,000 a day.

E-mail accessibility is fading fast for everyone. In the future, Gates believes that the only hook that will get an unfamiliar e-mail through is an outright bribe. "Eventually, there will be an approach where strangers who want to get someone's attention will have to say if they are willing to pay to get someone's attention," the newspaper quoted Gates as saying. "The person who reads the mail will have folders with the amounts marked on them. When you read a message you can decide to cancel the charge if you decide it was really worth reading for free."

There is nothing magic in e-mail that will save us from the info-glut. In fact, once the novelty wears off, an e-mail message will be the most difficult of all communication to put a hook or spin on. There is no envelope that can be handwritten or printed; there is no recording of your emotional tone as with voice mail; there is no visual image, as there is on a fax. E-mail is sure to change to a more visual medium—probably soon—but for now there is only who the e-mail is from, the time, and a few words' worth of space in the subject line.

The subject line is of extreme importance. Leaving it blank is likely to get your message ignored; remember that if your recipient is on a commercial service, they may be charged for just opening their e-mail. A blank or "unknown" subject line hardly seems worth paying to open.

If you're responding to the recipient's e-mail, *do not* put "your mail" in the subject line. Although you might think this is an authority flag, as it is in voice mail, the problem is that people may receive dozens, if not hundreds, of e-mails with a subject line that says "your mail."

If you're able to get someone to open your e-mail, then most standard spins will be applicable, but keep them short and send them to the right people. With the ease of sending e-mail, the old spin of "copying in" higher-ups to add authority can backfire, as Jack Montgomery points out:

You can copy your bosses several times removed. And you can over-inform them, and annoy them. There's an aspect of politics in it. We can all see who's the corporate suck-up, because he's the one that's got to copy three bosses above him every time. And you watch his stuff or her stuff and you see the style change depending on how high he or she's decided to copy it. It makes you look fatuous to send little things to big people.

Finally, you should realize that e-mail isn't private. A survey in *Macworld* indicated that 30 percent of companies that employ more than 1,000 people read their employees' e-mail. Many companies keep every message for years. Lawsuits have been won after experts have tracked down old e-mail messages recorded on computer tape languishing in the corporate archives. Throwing paper in your waste basket will send it to a landfill or a recycling plant in a matter of days, where it will never reappear. E-mail, on the other hand, can be pulled off a hard drive that has been entirely erased, reformatted, and rewritten.

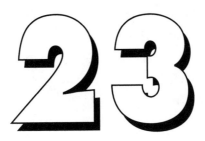

Presentation Spin

Presentations, whether they involve audiovisual setups or just a verbal presentation, can use nearly all the spin methods described in this book. But there is one effect that I should point out: nonstop presentations of any kind decrease an audience's time to think and increase its reliance on feeling. In short, an audience will be more spinable.

Neil Postman, in his book *Amusing Ourselves to Death: Public Discourse in the Age of Show Business*, describes television and radio in a way that applies equally to a rapid-fire business presentation: "Facts push other facts into and then out of consciousness at speeds that neither permit nor require evaluation."

This effect of facts pushing facts also means that nothing will stay in the audience's memory for long. Once an audience is accustomed to replacing one idea with the next, you'll have trouble making one stick. If you want your audience to retain detailed information, hand it out on paper.

This is why the most effective speakers don't bother with a lot of facts. Instead, they work to achieve a positive association between themselves and their audience and to illustrate simple points with evocative and expressive stories. As we'll see next, the story is really at the heart of the spin that persuades us most.

Original Spin: The Story

The story is the most ancient and pervasive method that humans use to communicate messages and show perspective. All cultures tell stories; from the Inuit of Greenland to the American engineers of IBM, people guide their audiences through experiences they create with words. It's so natural to turn *events* into stories (like the time you won the big account) that it's easy to forget that you can—and should—forge *information* into stories, too.

While facts can convince your audience's thinking brain, a good story will convince their feeling brain. "When you want to persuade somebody of something," says Tom Harrison, "you need facts, because facts establish your credibility. They establish that you're an expert. But facts alone are really boring. You need facts plus emotion. Facts plus emotion equals persuasion. And the emotion comes from the anecdotes."

Make It Live

A good story makes ideas come alive. To tell one that rouses your audience's emotions—whether that story is about a person, a product, or an idea—you've got to apply the basic principles of drama, which are:

Conflict. It's rule number one, and if you listen closely to a bad storyteller, you'll spot their failure immediately. A bad story is, "this happened, and then this happened." A good story sets up a conflict, whether it's two people battling it out or two theories being tested for their accuracy. And that conflict can't be resolved peacefully; one must win and one must lose. Compromises work well in life, but they're lousy in stories. Finally, something of value must be at stake in the conflict, or who cares? The most common kind of conflict in business is The Problem versus The Problem Solvers who try to conquer it.

Characters. People, ideas, or forces that conflict are the characters of your story. Erase from your mind the idea that you're going to have to make Ned from accounting sound colorful just because you want to use him in a story—that's not what character is about. What's important is that a character—whether it's Ned, your theory, or the falling price of aluminum—can carry the conflict. If Ned can believably struggle against the falling price of aluminum, and if the falling price can believably struggle against Ned, then you've got strong characters. Typically, characters are one or more good guys or forces (the protagonists) and one or more bad guys or forces (the antagonists).

Plot. If a conflict just sits there, there's no story. The characters must fight each other to win, and how that happens is the plot. The fundamental components of a plot include a beginning, in which the conflict is established; a middle, in which the struggle takes place; and an end, in which the protagonist wins or loses.

Also important is the idea of rising action, which means that the protagonist tries to win, has a setback, tries harder, has a bigger setback, gives it an all-out effort and is all but defeated when a tiny sliver of hope is suddenly turned into triumph.

Let's look at an example. In his book *Love & Profit: The Art of Caring Leadership*, James A. Autry makes the point that sometimes you've got to do what seems wrong to be right. He does it by telling this story:

Consider the news story a few years ago of the old, experienced captain of a Lockheed 1011 jumbo jet who, after taking off from San Francisco, could not get the nose down. He tried everything within reason, even putting his feet against the control column and pushing with all the strength he and his co-pilot could muster. The nose continued upward toward a sure stall. The engines simply would not have enough power to keep the big plane climbing at such a steep angle.

Just at the point when other pilots might only have hoped for a miracle, the captain pulled back the throttles, reducing engine power. On the face of it, this was madness, an action so precisely opposite of accepted flying technique that 95 percent of all the pilots in the world would have judged it suicide. Who but a madman would reduce power in the face of a stall?

Everyone knows the result. The nose, responding to less power for some reason, lowered, and did it quickly enough to avert a stall. The pilot was able to nurse the plane back to San Francisco, a major deficiency was discovered, all other L1011s were repaired, and, I'm sure, many lives were saved.

The captain explained, "When you try everything that's supposed to work and it doesn't work, the only thing left is what's not supposed to work."

Autry set up the conflict: the pilot against the stubborn nose of the plane. He describes the struggle and near defeat of the protagonist when the combined strength of the pilot and the co-pilot wouldn't budge the nose. He presents the last, unlikely hope—reducing power—and the victory that ensues. And finally, he tacks on the pilot's quote, which is the moral of his story.

In case you think Autry's story had the dramatic elements built into it and all he did was relay them, I'll retell the story drained of its drama:

Consider the news story a few years ago of the Lockheed 1011 jumbo jet with a mechanical malfunction that caused the nose to rise, a situation pilots found could be corrected by reducing power instead of the recommended procedure of increasing power. In the incident, the pilot discovered the effectiveness of the unorthodox maneuver after first attempting the usual correction. This allowed the plane to be brought back under control and returned to the airport, where repairs were made to this and other Lockheed 1011s. The pilot credited experimentation as the key to the solution to the problem.

Pretty Dull. The point of the story—that sometimes you've got to try something insane—is still there, but there's no impact left.

How to Use a Story

There are two ways to use a story in business communication. One is to make a point, the way Autry did above, with an unrelated but illustrative story. The other is to tell a story about your subject. Let's look at how to use an illustrative story first.

The benefit of an illustrative story is that you can present your ideas without raising audience resistance, even if you suspect they'll disagree. People are not inclined to object to a story because you're just relating something that happened. The story is about someone else, not them, yet to make sense of it they will have to experience it in their imagination.

To achieve that effect, you need to choose a story that has the same "shape" on the process level as your idea, but one with a different content. The shape of Autry's story conformed to the process he was talking about: trying conventional wisdom and then abandoning it to make progress. Imagine if he had told a story of pilots who had *accidentally* reduced power and saved the plane. He still might have claimed this shows that you have to try what seems absurd to get results. But since the pilots in his story hadn't tried, his audience wouldn't conceive of themselves as trying, either. The story's shape would have been different. Accidents are one thing; effort is another.

The "What," "So What," and "Now What"

Stories about your subject are fundamentally different from illustrative stories. They should be dramatic—all stories should be—but they should be driven by causation, function, and applicability. Your story should present a problem that needs to be solved, explain the values at stake, and show how your solution solves the problem—the "What," "So what," and "Now what" structure. If your idea has been put into action, you can tell what happened, then project into the future. If your idea hasn't yet been applied, you can only project—but do it as a story. Tom Harrison fires up his audience's imagination from the beginning:

> I often use the word *imagine* to start off. "Imagine if we did . . ." It's almost that by saying that you engage the right part of their brain. "Imagine. . . ." Bing. They do. And you let them dream with you a little bit. "Imagine if we applied that here. Imagine if we were able to take this and do this and do this and do this." Now they understand what you just told them. It went from being interesting information at best to being useful and applicable.

If you're analyzing rather than proscribing, use a detective story form: you're the detective (the protagonist), brilliantly solving a perplexing riddle (the antagonist). Mysteries are known as either open, where you don't know who did it, or closed, where you know who did it, but you don't know how the detective will solve the case. As I said earlier, suspense is not usually a good idea in business—your audience has to know where you're going—and for that reason, your mystery should be closed. State your conclusions, then tell the amazing story of how you conquered the unknown.

Story Shift

The drama of stories is often so compelling that your audience's attention will be distracted from the actual content of your information. That effect can come in handy if you need it, but it's also one you might accidentally trigger when you don't intend to.

Ronald Reagan's advisers smoothly used "Story Shift" spin when in 1981 David Stockman, the administration's economic guru, challenged the accuracy of his boss's budget numbers. Reagan's public relations people intentionally played up the drama of the story to try to avoid the content of what Stockman had said: Here was a disobedient son betraying his loyal father. Once Stockman apologized, the drama was resolved. The importance of what he had said—that Reagan's budget was built on sand—evaporated.

The classic preface to a story shift is to simply say, "The real story here is . . ." and then move into the realm of drama—a story of betrayal, loyalty, fear, or courage. What's important is that the shift is to a fundamental, dramatic human issue. Union leaders, for example, often appeal to their members by shifting from the content of a particular contract to the drama of using solidarity to challenge exploitation. In your response to another department's criticism of your idea you might explain that the real story is one of interdepartmental jealously.

Dramatic spin can also overshadow content when you don't want it to. In November of 1994, when consumers discovered that Intel corporation's Pentium computer chip was flawed, Intel tried to stay focused on the issue—that only a minuscule percent of all Pentium users would ever encounter the problem, and for those who did, the company would replace the chip. But computer owners were suspicious, and the story quickly shifted to the consumers' betrayed trust and the company's continuing arrogance. Impelled only by the escalating drama (in truth, almost no one actually had problems with the chip), Intel was eventually forced to offer a new chip to any customer who asked.

A story can be implicit in even the smallest part of communication. The name of the early database software dBase II implied that it was an improvement over dBase I. You might have assumed the product had been successful enough to have been around awhile, and perhaps that most of the bugs had been worked out. In fact, there never was a dBase I. The name dBase II was created to spin a little story.

Stories that are compressed into a single word or phrase are what I call labels—small bits of information that can produce powerful spin.

25

Put On a Label

In one sense, it's impossible to say anything without adding spin; spin is built into our language. Every word we use carries a connotation, and unless you're aware of it, you can use words that spin your meaning far away from where you want it to be. Labels packed with heuristic power vie for dominance in the media daily—*pro-life* or *anti-abortion*; *military advisers* or *troops*; *downsizing* or *layoffs*. You might think that if you're cutting a budget, you're cutting a budget, yet *Time* magazine recently reported that Congressman John Kaisch "pleaded with reporters not even to use the word *cuts* in describing his Medicare proposals." His spin—the perspective he was trying to reveal by avoiding the word *cuts*—was that Medicare spending would still rise in the future, just not as fast as it used to.

Labels Help Define How We Think and Feel. Take the example of the medical body scanner that was developed to paint an electronic picture of a patient's internal organs. It was a breakthrough diagnostic tool, but there was one problem: patients recoiled at being exposed to something called a Nuclear Magnetic Resonance (NMR) scanner. Explaining that the machine had nothing at all to do with nuclear fusion or radioactivity didn't help. When the name was changed to Magnetic Resonance Imaging (MRI) scanner, patients' fears disappeared. The machine wasn't changed, and both descriptions are accurate (it works by using magnetism to vibrate the body's hydrogen nuclei), but "magnetic" sounded familiar and friendly, while "nuclear" sounded like you'd be shot through with deadly rays.

Bad labels can hide in seemingly innocent phrases. One nonprofit company found that calling a department "Volunteer Recruitment" gave people the idea that if you called to volunteer, you'd be "recruited"—perhaps for something you didn't want to do. The department name was changed to "Volunteer Opportunities," which, after all, is what they were.

Mistakes in labeling terms usually happens because we tend to label things from our orientation instead of our audience's. As far as the nonprofit company mentioned above was concerned, they needed to recruit volunteers, so that's what they called the department, failing to see things from the potential volunteers' point of view.

Controlling the spin of labels begins at the micro-level. When you're composing a message, it's easy to forget that you don't necessarily have to use the labels everyone else is using to define a situation or problem.

An annual report from an investment fund that I have on my desk offers an example of good labeling. In 1994, mutual funds took a beating; there were no two ways about it. Yet the fund's report describes its year as a "pause from the rapid growth of recent years." A *pause* is an accurate description that offers a new perspective: it reminds investors that 1994 was one bad year out of several good ones and that mutual funds are designed to be *long-term* investments. Labels such as a *loss*, *drop*, or *slide* would imply a failure to meet *short-term* investment goals.

What's in a Name?

Naming things that everyone recognizes, such as medical scanners, departments, or investment returns is one way to use labeling to control spin. An even more powerful way is to name what hasn't yet been recognized as a separately existing process, effect, or thing.

This technique is at the heart of much of what eventually becomes buzz in our world. Alvin Toffler called our reaction to accelerating change *future shock*. He put a name on a phenomenon we knew was happening but didn't recognize. *Reengineering*, *team building*, and *time management* are names for processes that we all did but that took on special meaning once they were named and defined. The label *information superhighway* (both a label and a metaphor) has set the spin for millions of people who now picture electronic connectivity as something as public and inevitable as the country's road system.

If you are having trouble describing a process or idea or find yourself repeating an awkward phrase, you probably have an opportunity to coin a new term. It's an opportunity you shouldn't take lightly. If you're writing a major report, devote a few days to considering the names or terms you'll use for the major concepts. How easy will they be for people to remember? How evocative are they? Imagine the result if the label you invent passes from your company to your industry at large. Does it still work?

The best names are short, unique, and vivid. I once needed a name for the weekly report my department issued that detailed the production status of various publications. We could have called it *Publication Production Status Report*, or some such thing, but instead we named it *Where It's At*, which, after all, is what people wanted to know about their publication. The report might have been just as useful without the name, but the name made it fun to talk about and refer to. After a few months, other departments were issuing their own reports, entitled *Where It's At for Data Processing* or *Where It's At for Product Development*. The concept of a *Where It's At* report became generic, based on my department's model.

Naming a concept or process is especially powerful, because if you named it, you are the authority on it. If you coin the term the *Christmas-tree effect*, which you define as the tendency of some of your company's projects to look beautiful for a week before they turn brown and ugly, then people will seek your advice on what to do about it.

Labels can also help untangle overlapping or intermingled ideas. One executive told me that their team was wracking their brains trying to figure out how to assemble a proposal for a particular client. This client, they knew, would demand too much service for too little compensation. Finally, one team member hit on a solution—a complement of labels. She suggested they propose four levels of service for four different fee structures. To label them, she borrowed terms from frequent flyer programs: the *bronze*, *silver*, *gold*, and *platinum* levels. Both sides still wrangled over money—the client wanted platinum service at bronze prices—but the labels gave definition to the bargaining.

Scour your message for words that carry the most meaning and imagine what other words you might use or invent. One way to create an effective label, as I did with the *Christmas-tree effect*, is to draw upon a deep power in our language: the metaphor.

Make a Metaphor

Just as the connotation of words is built into our language, so are metaphors. They live in words we take for granted. If I say I'm under pressure, I'm not talking about the atmosphere pressing on my skin; I'm talking about responsibilities metaphorically pressing on my consciousness. Words are constantly gathering meaning by being used metaphorically. Not long ago a virus was something only organisms could get; now a computer can catch one, too. The language of business is filled with its own metaphoric words and phrases: *launching* a project, *chewing out* a staff member, *wrapping up* a deal. But to control metaphorical spin, you have to do two things: Carefully choose the metaphors you use and create new ones that express your meaning.

Some common metaphors you might use unthinkingly will spin your meaning in a dangerous direction. Do you mean:

"I'll go over it" or "I'll give it my full attention"?

"I'll put it through channels" or "I'll make sure it gets approved"?

"Let's close the deal" or "Let's come to an agreement"?

With some thought, you can also add common metaphors to your communication that will help guide your message. Do you mean:

"I'll call and let them know you're coming" or "I'll smooth the way for you"?

"I'll ask them back at the office" or "I'll tap our experts."

"I'll ask them to start" or "I'll get them up to speed."

You can add the spin of metaphor by adopting words from other places to put in your communication. For example, you can emphasize your expertise by borrowing images and words from other professions:

Instead of "I'll translate the technical language," you could say, "I'll decode this."

Instead of "This will take some research into the archives," you could say, "This will take an archeological dig."

Instead of "This will take some careful rewriting," you could say, "This will take some reconstructive surgery."

Get Vivid

Effective metaphors call up associations with a universal truth and yet are still vivid and precise. That's why tired sports metaphors are such failures. "To say that our company is going to score a touchdown because we've got a great quarterback is so general that there is no precision," says Jack Montgomery. "The only universal law called upon is the idea of effective leaders, and that's too general to command any attention." Throughout our interview, Jack used metaphors to paint vivid pictures. He described an angry client as "full of steam," and an executive who made a casual speech as delivering the "Jimmy Carter put-on-the-cardigan kind of thing." The metaphors made his messages memorable.

But metaphors have more than memory power. They can dramatically improve the effectiveness of communication. Social psychologists Anthony Pratkanis and Elliot Aronson took on the task of trying to improve a utility company's efforts to get homeowners to take an interest-free loan to insulate their homes. The company's success rate had been only 15 percent. The psychologists looked at the problem and decided that what was lacking were strong metaphors, vividly told. They advised the company's energy auditors to try telling this to homeowners:

Look at all the cracks around that door! It may not seem like much to you, but if you were to add up all the cracks around each of these doors, you'd have the equivalent of a hole the circumference of a basketball. Suppose someone poked a hole the size of a basketball in your living room wall. Think for a moment about all the heat that you'd be losing from a hole that size—you'd want to patch that hole in your wall, wouldn't you? That's exactly what weather-stripping does. And your attic totally lacks insulation. We professionals called that a "naked" attic. It's as if your home is facing winter not just without an overcoat but without any clothing at all! You wouldn't let your young kids run around outside in the winter time without clothes on, would you? It's the same with your attic.

When homeowners heard this speech, they signed up in droves: 61 percent had their houses insulated. One of the reasons the metaphors were so effective is because they used situations and images that were familiar to their audience: big holes the size of a basketball and naked children running through the snow.

A financial executive I talked to also makes sure he uses something his audience can grasp:

I've given many internal presentations that describe the kind of work we do here in this department, which can be pretty esoteric sometimes. And the technique for bringing that across is to try to boil it down to examples of everyday finances, where you talk about somebody's checking account as opposed to the corporate coffers. You talk about their home mortgage as an analogy for a very complicated project financing.

To work, an audience must be familiar with the basis of your analogy: If you compare launching a project to planning a Himalayan mountain climbing assault on K-2, your metaphor might be clever but it won't win many people in your audience, unless you're speaking to a group of mountaineers.

Metaphors work as spin because they show your audience a new perspective by comparing one thing to another. There is another technique that, instead of emphasizing the similarity of two ideas, emphasizes the difference. Instead of revealing a new viewpoint, it reveals a new world; it's the technique I call the "Paradigm Shift."

27

Shift the Paradigm

Kit Rachlis, now an editor at the *Los Angeles Times Magazine*, remembers a day when, as a young freelance critic for the *Village Voice*, he got a call from his editor. Kit had struggled to get his review of a musical performance to his boss, editor Bob Christgau, just before the Thanksgiving holiday. With the piece safely on Bob's desk, Kit was up to his elbows in stuffing on turkey day when the phone rang. It was Bob. Bob complimented Kit on the review, saying it was really very good. And then came the shift. "It's good now, but with a little more work it could be *great*. And I assume you're interested in greatness." Kit could only answer yes. "Good," Bob replied, "Can you rewrite it and get it to me by Friday?"

Greatness wasn't just a whole new ball game, it was a new stadium. Writing good articles was just part of the nine-to-five, holidays-not-included job. But greatness—well, there would be other Thanksgivings.

A "Paradigm Shift" spin is when you move the criteria for evaluating your message to a new, usually grander, scale. Suddenly, all bets are off. The old rules don't apply, and everything is in flux. The "Paradigm Shift" is a risk, but the results can be breathtaking.

What distinguishes a new paradigm from an old one is that its new features create a new way of thinking about a common idea. A discount store is a common idea; a "club" store with limited membership, security door checks to eliminate inventory shrinkage, warehouse shelving, no service people except for cashiers—that's a new paradigm. A series of new ice-cream flavors is a common idea; gourmet flavors studded with candy and fruit, with wild names like Cherry Garcia, produced by counter-culture types Ben and Jerry—that's a new paradigm.

A new paradigm doesn't have to be the basis of a new, multimillion dollar industry; it just has to evoke a different mindset than what has gone before. In *What Color Is Your Parachute?*, author Richard Nelson Bolles uses a "Paradigm Shift" spin to suggest that in a job search you go to a company not as a job-beggar, but as a resource person:

You're not visiting an employer in order to get him or her to do *you* a big favor. If you've done your homework, you know you can be part of the solution there, and not part of the problem. Therefore you're going in to see this employer in order that you may do a favor *for each other*. That's not an arrogant posture for you to take. It *is* the truth, and it can be stated very quietly but confidently. You are coming to see this employer, in order to make an oral proposal, followed hopefully by a written proposal, of what *you* can do for *them*.

You will perceive immediately what a switch this is from the way *most* job-hunters approach an employer!

Creating a new paradigm can't be a halfhearted effort, otherwise it'll sound like a bad euphemism. You can't put an answering machine on a phone and call it an automated customer-service technical resource hot line. To work, a new paradigm has to be a new vision, an innovation, or a transformation of the usual. It requires more torque than most spins because the perspective you're hoping to show your audience is from a radical angle. But because it's new and different, it can sometimes escape the usual criticism.

For example, suppose you want to talk your boss into subscribing to an on-line database service you've found useful. Put that way, your idea would fit into the usual request for equipment and services. It might be rejected if it were evaluated on its return on the investment. But what if in your proposal you named it an Information Resource Center (and referred to it in speech as "the IRC")? Creating your IRC might include gathering books to a central location, where you would also install a new computer supplied with reference works on CD-ROM and linked to the new database and the Internet. Seen this way, your suggestion is a new paradigm; It's more like establishing a new mini-department than asking for a new purchase.

Spinning a new paradigm starts by denying that your idea is what it might seem to be. "I'm not talking about adding a copy machine," you say, "I'm talking about creating on-demand publishing for all our company brochures," or, "I don't mean a staff of sales people; I mean consultants who have expertise in their field and who also represent our company." What you choose to deny is important, because it actually tells your audience something about your idea. If you only say, "I'm not talking about business as usual; I'm talking about a whole new way of creating products," then you have failed to communicate anything worthwhile. There is no base from which the new paradigm can spring. By saying your idea is *not* something, you imply that it is *like* that thing, only better.

A new paradigm is an accumulation of features that fit together in an integrated way to coalesce into a reconception of the usual, as we saw with the paradigm of "club" stores and Ben and Jerry's ice cream. Any one of their individual features would not be enough to propel them into a new paradigm, but together the total effect is greater than the sum of its parts. Don't try a "New Paradigm" spin unless your idea has enough new features to pull it off. Going through the exercise of developing this spin has the added benefit of inspiring you to come up with good ideas just to plug into the spin.

Suggesting a new paradigm is often the best way to counter a proposal you don't like. If Randy wants a meeting from 10:00 a.m. to noon, which you'd have to miss, don't just argue over the time. You might present a new paradigm: "I think we need something different from just another meeting. Let's get everybody to pile in the company van and drive to that new restaurant where we can have a mini-retreat. We can cover the information, get free of the office distractions, and get to know each other better at the same time." Now the event is no longer just a meeting; it's a mini-retreat and has several features that make it so.

Because offering a new paradigm can be threatening to some people, you should always have a backup spin that's safer, although even if your new paradigm is rejected, it's done its job. That's because in shifting back to a suggestion that's old-paradigm (perhaps your same idea, minus one or two features), you're making a concession, which engages reciprocity in your audience and will make them want to offer you a concession in return. If your mini-retreat idea is nixed, you might say, "Well, okay, let's just walk across the street and have a normal lunch meeting at the usual spot." All that's really missing is the van ride, yet Randy hears you reluctantly giving up the idea of a mini-retreat, a reciprocity spin that might trigger his agreement.

Use Numbers

It's shocking to realize that 50 percent of the American population has a better-than-average ability in math, yet half the people in this country are below average in understanding statistical analysis. This alarming fact may be because although 50 percent of Americans are above-average in education, one out of two is sub-average in the ability to perform simple calculations.

For example, what would you estimate are the odds against Tom Hanks being awarded an Oscar two years in a row, as he was in 1993 for *Philadelphia* and again in 1994 for *Forrest Gump*? You might be surprised to learn that they were 62,500,000,000,000 to one.

Did you spot the spin in the two paragraphs above? Neither uses false information, but each has been spun to show a particular perspective. And each shows that, by controlling the assumptions that underlay numbers, you can control the spin.

All About Averages

All numerical data has assumptions behind it. For example, an *average* is an attempt to measure the "central tendency" of a set of data. There are three ways to do that: the median average, the mean average, and the mode average. Which one best represents the central tendency of the data is often a matter of opinion.

The median average is the point at which half the samples are above and half are below. That's the average I used in the startling statements I made in the first paragraph. I didn't have to look up any math scores to know that half the population is above the median in math abilities and half below—that's the *definition* of a median average. As long as you're talking about a median average, half the population is always above average and half below in any generalized value you care to name: half are taller than average, half shorter; half are below average in wealth, half above.

The other two kinds of averages are the *mean*, which would be found in the example above by adding everyone's math scores together and dividing by the number of people, and the *mode*, which is simply the score that most people got.

Depending on the distribution of the data, the three averages can be vastly different from each other. If you have five people who make $10,000 a year, four people who make $20,000 a year, and one who makes a million, the median average income of the group would be $20,000; the mean average would be $113,000; and the mode average would be $10,000. Which one best represents the central tendency of the data? Take your pick.

Just as important as *how* you average is *who* you average. Even before a group of people or numbers are boiled down to an average, assumptions go into choosing the larger group in the first place.

When Intel's Pentium computer chip was found to be flawed, two statistics hit the press that were supposed to describe how computer users would be affected. Intel estimated how often the bug would bug the "typical user using a spreadsheet program." IBM estimated how often it would pester "an average spreadsheet user." Intel said it would happen once every 27,000 years. IBM said it would hit every 24 *days*. How were users different? We can only guess that to Intel, a "typical user using a spreadsheet" was someone who didn't use a spreadsheet that often, whereas to IBM, an "average spreadsheet user" was someone who used a spreadsheet every day. Just for your amusement, I might point out that those estimates differ by roughly 32,400,000 percent—quite a spread for just choosing a different group of folks to average.

When you're going to make your case with an average, think carefully about what you might include or exclude that will change the result of the average. For example, let's say you're trying to talk your boss into paying your way to a seminar. You want to make the case that the average amount of money spent on each employee in your department for seminars is small—but there are two people who've just spent two weeks each being trained to use the new software, and they throw off the average. The answer is to simply exclude them from your average, and say so. "Except for Bill and Judy, who had to get trained for that new software, the average we spend on each person for education is only $35 a year." That is accurate, yet keeps your spin and makes your point.

Imagine the Odds

Assumptions also affect odds. I came up with my figure about Tom Hanks' Academy Award chances based on an unusual assumption: that anyone in America might win an Oscar in any given year. I can defend that assumption by pointing out that for a nonactor to win the award is not unheard of. It happened in 1946, when Harold Russell won best supporting actor for his portrayal of what he was—a disabled war veteran—in *The Best Years of Our Lives*. Russell wasn't an actor and had had no intentions of becoming one until director William Wyler discovered him. So my premise is that for Tom Hanks to win in a single year, he has to beat out everyone else in America—approximately a 250-million-to-one shot. Now to do it two years in a row, I multiplied 250 million times 250 million to get one chance in more than 62 trillion.

Although my spin is exaggerated, it's the same spin you might use if you said, "There are nine other agencies besides us trying to get this account. Our chances are one in ten." Your underlying assumption, which would create the spin, is that all the agencies are equally matched.

How Many?

On the other end of the numbers game from assumption is the spin of interpretation. The problem (and opportunity for spin) comes in trying to sum up results that are hard to sum up. Let's say you have the results of a survey in which you asked clients how satisfied they were with your company's service, and they look like this:

Very dissatisfied: 12 percent
Somewhat dissatisfied: 28 percent
Satisfied: 30 percent

Very satisfied: 14 percent

Extremely satisfied: 16 percent

From these figures you could say that 60 percent of your clients thought you were doing a reasonable job or better. Or you could say that 70 percent of your clients thought your company was just adequate or worse. Either interpretation would be true, but the spin in each case is entirely different.

Two common ways to express quantity are as a percentage or as an absolute number, and each can be the better spin depending on the situation. Sometimes a percentage will be most impressive expressed as a percentage: "Forty percent of our staff have a Master's degree in their field" is a true and impressive statement about a start-up company employing five people, two of whom have Master's. On the other hand, if sales of your company's toothpicks have gone up only 3 percent, you might want to express that in absolute numbers, saying, "Our company has sold more than 50 million more toothpicks this year than last." A treasury executive at a Fortune 25 oil company notes that this spin is a favorite of some of the oil company's critics. "In our business, if there's a spill, God forbid, environmentalists much prefer to talk about things in gallons than barrels, because the number is 42 times larger."

Putting a value in concrete terms can make it more impressive, a spin I think of as "to the moon and back" as in, "If our profits were laid out in nickels, they'd reach to the moon and back." When I was hired to try to convince Los Angeles commuters to carpool to reduce traffic, my department wanted to come up with an image of how bad traffic was. We found that if all the rush-hour traffic was put on one freeway, it would fill the freeway for miles. Not quite to the moon, but impressive nonetheless.

Even within the realm of percentages, there is room to spin. There is a big difference, for example, between *percent* and *percentage points*. If your profit margin has shrunk from 10 percent to 5 percent, you might want to say it's "fallen 5 percentage points." If your profit margin has grown from 5 percent to 10 percent, you might want to say it's "increased by 100 percent." If someone suggests your prices are too high, you might say your profit margin "is only 10 percent above cost." However, if a potential investor wants to know how you're doing, you would probably want to use annual return on investment, which can be much different. For example, if you make a 10 percent profit and sell out your inventory each week, your annual return on investment is 520 percent.

Comparisons

You can also spin different perspectives by what you compare numbers to. You can compare your profits this year to last year's profits, or you can compare them to the average profit over the last ten years, which might give completely different results. Your audience may not know that 5 percent is a terrific response for direct-mail advertising (3 percent is typical). They might think that sounds pathetic, unless you tell them otherwise. One executive I spoke to saw a poor soul ground into the dirt for failing to put a number in context:

I was just in a meeting where the CEO says, *"You spent fifty thousand dollars on this project?"* The perspective of the person doing it was, "I'm going to get a raise because I *only* spent fifty thousand dollars on this project." The CEO was *furious*. That person needed to come in and say, "The best news about this is we spent fifty grand—I know that's a lot of money, but let me tell you why we got a hundred thousand dollars worth of stuff for fifty."

The technique is to make a big expenditure seem small compared to what you got for it. A treasury executive at a large corporation told me he often finds himself before the board of directors, people who aren't easily impressed by many numbers under a billion. He often needs to use spin to make small numbers seem more important. He does it by putting his fish in a smaller pond, which makes it seem bigger:

Is a million dollars a lot or a little? In trying to get someone to pay attention to this million dollar problem, when they're accustomed to dealing with 50 million dollar problems, you say "Look, this is a million dollar problem. The reason that's a lot to be concerned about is that although it's lost in the rounding of our bottom line, I want you to realize it's a full 50 percent of our widget budget."

If you have a lot of numbers to deliver, you won't have time to offer a full explanation of each one, but you should use a few words to set the spin. In the direct mail example above, you might say something like "The response was *extremely strong* at a 5 percent response rate." Or you might say, "The response was *slightly less than expected* at 2.6 percent."

Avoid words that are too obviously loaded, such as "an incredible two thirds" or "a measly two thirds." You want to guide the figure into either the "that sounds good" or the "that sounds bad" part of your audience's mind; anything more will trigger suspicion.

Let's assume that the number you're spinning is 68 percent. Here are some sample phrases:

To emphasize that number as large:

More than two thirds

More than two out of three

Over two thirds

Nearly seven out of ten

To emphasize that number as small:

Less than three quarters

Fewer than three out of four

Under three quarters

If a number is important enough, you may need to put it in context *twice*. You might say, "Only slightly more than two thirds of our suppliers provide us with products that consistently perform up to specifications. Looked at another way, nearly one out of three of our products is unreliable."

What's in a Number?—A Name

Numbers have personality. Notice how often numbers are used in names: a Boeing 727, a Mazda 280Z, Baskin-Robbins 31 Flavors. H. J. Heinz, the founder of Heinz foods, was already selling more than fifty-seven varieties of condiments when he registered that slogan as a trademark. He simply liked the number. An odd number like that tells a story: it implies accuracy. Since it's precise, it must not be an estimate. Because it's concrete, it's easier to visualize than, say, "dozens of varieties." And it's distinctive, like the name that it has become.

In business communication, you can use this effect to make a report more memorable. If you're going to make a point-by-point argument, you might title the report "Marketing in Ecuador: 17 Challenges." You might start a talk by calling it your five-point plan to reduce overhead. If you're describing a project in conversation and you want to tie it to a previously successful project, you might say, "Think of this as Turbotech, part two."

The Sudden Twist

Although it's rare, you may sometime get the chance to use one of the most effective kinds of spin, what I call the "Sudden Twist" spin. The reason it's rare is that the circumstances have to be just right for it to be delivered well. But when you can do it, the "Sudden Twist" will persuade your audience like no other spin.

The spin uses the same principle as all spin—you set up the rules for judging an issue, and then you present your argument, which happens to meet the rules nicely. It's dramatic because at first, you seem to accept rules that *doom* your argument, and then you twist those rules at the very last moment, revealing your point of view to be the correct one after all. Let's look at some examples from politics, where the "Sudden Twist" has become an art.

In Ronald Reagan's reelection campaign, his first debate with Walter Mondale was a disaster. He rambled, got his facts wrong, and seemed to drift in and out of lucidity. One observer claimed he drooled. The media began asking questions. Everyone wanted to know: Was the seventy-three-year-old Reagan—the oldest president in history—competent to lead?

When it came time for the second debate, Reagan knew he would have to answer the age question. A reporter from the panel asked Reagan point blank if he thought he was up to the job. Reagan responded, "I will not make my age an issue in this campaign. I am not going to exploit, for political purposes, my opponent's youth and inexperience." Reporters chuckled, and the president's approval rate shot up on the spot.

To deliver his spin, Reagan's first move was to seem to head into a nose-dive. By saying, "I will not make my age an issue in this campaign," he led everyone to believe he was going to stonewall. At that moment, reporters everywhere were no doubt ready to pounce. What did he mean *he* would not make his age an issue? It *already was* an issue—everyone knew that. By seeming to say he wouldn't discuss his age, Reagan looked as though he himself wasn't confident in his ability. This, of course, was all part of his masterful setup to part two of his spin—the part that turned all that reasoning on its head. "I am not going to exploit, for political purposes," he said, a wry smile beginning to cross his lips, "my opponent's youth and inexperience." A quick whiplash to the other side. Now, Reagan reminded everyone, there were positives to consider that come with age: wisdom and experience.

What makes the "Sudden Twist" work—and you can see it clearly in this example—is its quick and dramatic reversal. Think of how much weaker Reagan's argument would have been if he had gone straight to his point by saying, "I would like to point out that my years of service have provided me a breadth of experience my opponent cannot match." With no surprising switch, the audience would have had too much time to think of all the reasons that might not be true. Instead, by catching his audience off guard, Reagan's point seemed like a flash of insight; it had that quality of immediate understanding that we often get when we realize a new truth.

Here's how Reagan built his spin. When he was confronted with the age problem, he couldn't deny his age, and age was the criteria. In its simplest terms, the argument against him was young equals good, old equals bad. His first step was to look for criteria that would reverse that equation. Reagan found it by taking a hard look at all the associations we have with age and youth. He realized that age is associated with experience and wisdom; youth with inexperience and immaturity. Next, he needed to find the best way to set up his audience for the flip. He chose to use the form of a joke and to position the flip as a punch line. Besides making him look confident (you don't joke about what worries you), it demonstrated that he wasn't senile; in fact, he seemed witty and sharp. The joke form had the added advantage of discouraging close scrutiny. It was just a joke, but it made his point.

The "Sudden Twist" is often delivered as a joke for just these reasons. In 1985, John D. Rockefeller used a "Sudden Twist' joke to counter the grumbling that he had been elected senator only because his wealth let him buy so much advertising. At a formal affair at the Washington Press Foundation, he faced a hostile audience: a roomful of working reporters who could ill afford the price of the fancy dinner. When it came time for him to speak, he began this way: "To those of you who had to fork over seventy-five bucks for your tickets, don't feel so bad. It cost me twelve million to get here tonight."

Once again, it was the one-two punch. In his setup, Rockefeller seemed to be leaving himself wide open for potshots. "To those of you who had to fork over seventy-five bucks for your tickets, don't feel so bad." That was easy for a multimillionaire to say, the reporters probably thought. Was he going to tell them it was well worth the money? How would he know? He had money to burn. Then came the twist. "It cost me twelve million to get here tonight." The sudden new perspective that Rockefeller revealed was that price is relative. Seventy-five dollars is a lot for a reporter, and twelve million is a lot for a millionaire. It's all just part of sacrificing for what you want.

Once again, it's the surprising insight that is convincing. If Rockefeller had begun by saying, "You know, twelve million dollars may seem like a lot of money, but when you compare it to my overall assets . . ." it is doubtful he could have been heard above the reporters' roaring laughter.

To build this spin, Rockefeller looked at the criteria associated with spending money: what was positive, and what was negative. Focusing on the good, he understood that everyone spends money to get what they want; the trick was to show that the expenditure was reasonable and not somehow unfair.

Despite its name, the "Sudden Twist" doesn't always need to be a one-liner; the suddenness of the twist is relative. If the setup took years, then the twist that takes place over a few months is still sudden. Bill Clinton used this spin throughout his campaign by reversing the public perception of the 1980s. To do it, he had to turn what looked like more than a decade of economic success into a record of bad policy. The *Los Angeles Times* noted that most Democrats had given up:

But Clinton did take on the 1980s, and he made it work where others had failed. For some time, liberals had argued that the decade's prosperity was illusory. The public never bought it. Clinton made a different argument: The 1980s were a success on the surface, but underneath was decay and neglect. We didn't invest in people or infrastructure, which is how you create real wealth. You've got some lovely towers there, Clinton said in effect, but they're built on sand.

Clinton didn't use the direct approach that had failed other liberals. He began by agreeing: Yes, many of us made a lot of money in the 1980s. Yes, we enjoyed tax cuts. And then the twist: But there's no such thing as a free lunch—what's been the real price? His answer: streets filled with the homeless and an enormous national debt.

It's a piece of spin that's become lodged in the conscience of many Americans; the 1980s are now usually depicted as the decade of greed. Clinton turned the criteria around, suggesting that these wonderful things might not be so great under closer inspection.

The "Sudden Twist" works around the office the same way it does in politics: with a setup and a quick reverse. One executive I talked to remembers a meeting in which the other side tried to bully her into making a decision on the spot. They had presented reams of research papers, fancy charts, and stacks of graphs. Their argument was that with all this material, the groundwork had been laid and it was time for action. Their equation was that thorough investigation equals a good decision. But my friend took that equation and applied it in a new way. If thoroughness was good, she'd jump on the bandwagon. "I can see that a lot of time and effort went into your plan," she said as her setup. They must have expected her to follow with a yes or no decision. Instead, she used their criteria to twist her spin: "And so I'm sure you can see that we'll need to put an equal amount of time and effort into our consideration."

If you're lucky, you can sometimes spin the very words of your opponent to reveal the new meaning of the criteria. Not long ago I was asked to help a company fight a front-page newspaper article that maligned them. The headline declared that their program was near collapse, and all kinds of financial improprieties were implied. One government official was quoted in the article as saying, "The [government] auditors said, in a nutshell, that they couldn't figure out what the hell was going on." If a good audit was the criteria, I thought, then let's look at that. In my research I discovered that for twenty years this company had undergone audits by Price Waterhouse and Peat Marwick—extremely reputable auditors—and that they had always passed with flying colors. In my setup, I agreed that good audits were certainly important. Then came the twist: I suggested that if the government's auditors "couldn't figure out what was going on," that said more about *the auditors* than it did about the company that was audited.

Jack Montgomery found himself in the unenviable position of telling his manufacturing customers that the chemical company he worked for was raising the prices of its raw supplies. And he sensed that in this case, a partial spin wouldn't mollify the manufacturers. "Death is to say, 'We haven't been making money this year. It's our turn,'" Jack told me. "Anything that's wounded wing won't work. People don't care about that."

Jack's company needed a 180-degree turn. To do it, they'd have to show that higher prices were good, not bad. When he took a good look at the consequences of continued low prices, he found the problem: Without getting a better price, Jack's company couldn't increase supply, which would hurt customers.

His setup was to agree with the unspoken accusation of his customers: yes, his company would be increasing its profits. And the twist—*But here's why*:

All throughout the recession things were so bad and we were making so little money we had to keep capacity down. We were running at tiny margins and not only did we not build any new plants, we consolidated products, shut down plants, and effectively reduced capacity. Now the only way we can continue to meet the capacity requirements of the industry is to have enough margin for reinvestment economics. [These price hikes are] going to enable us to make enough money to build the next plant, so that we don't run out of capacity, so that *you* don't run out of capacity and shut down *your* plant.

Suddenly those higher prices didn't look so bad. The "Sudden Twist" isn't always necessary and is often inadvisable. Nothing is more dangerous than a "Sudden Twist" that bombs. Because it begins with a setup that agrees with the opposing view, if the twist fails, then the opposing view is left even stronger. Not only that, but the spinner looks not like someone who's delivered a sudden new insight but as someone who tried to put one over on everybody. Don't try it unless you feel in your bones that the exact opposite view is strong, powerful, and is being ignored. If that's not the case, then use a subtler spin.

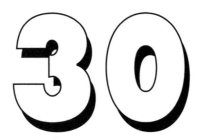

Disinformation

At the far end of spin, lying somewhere between spin and deceit, is the shady world of disinformation. Disinformation is leaving your audience with a belief that's not precisely accurate but not actually telling a lie. I'll describe the techniques and leave the ethics to you.

The most innocent kind of disinformation spin is possible because of the way our language works. By using a passive sentence construction instead of an active one, you can shift responsibility away from you and onto anonymous, unnamed people or forces. It's the difference between saying "I lost the Perkins account" and "The Perkins account was lost." In the case of taking credit for something good, you can claim some glory by including yourself, even if your only contribution was to be employed by your company at the time: "We won the Perkins account," instead of "The Perkins account was won" or "The company won the Perkins account." If you've got an angry client or customer on your hands, this kind of spin is essential. Beginning with a passive construction, you can acknowledge the problem but still frame it as an event far outside the company's usual operation. "That shouldn't have happened," you can say, and then, switching to the active form to emphasize your role in the solution, you can say, "I will make sure the problem is solved."

Using different sentence constructions, you can control the amount of spin in responsibility-taking statements. Here are six levels, going from highest to lowest:

"I made a mistake."
"We made a mistake."
"A mistake was made on our side."
"A mistake was made."
"There was a problem."
"A problem came up."

Notice how the first statement implies that you are completely responsible, whereas the last one makes it sound like the problem itself is somehow responsible—after all, it was the one that "came up."

Disinformation can go much farther than this, and there are no hard and fast rules I can give you on how or when to use it. Typically, a piece of disinformation isn't fundamental to the argument—in that case, it's clearly deception—but is used to trigger other forces, which you can then use to your advantage.

Lyndon Johnson once instructed an aide to spread a rumor about his opponent in an election. The aide protested that the rumor was an obvious lie, and that no one would believe it. "I know," replied Johnson, "but I want to see him *deny* it."

PART III

BUZZ:
A Good Word

When people use the word buzz, they usually mean an idea, rumor, or trend that's on everyone's mind. These are all examples of buzz, but a broader definition is needed to understand the real power of buzz. Buzz isn't just the latest news; buzz is any widely held opinion or belief. When buzz is new it may seem more important, but any idea, new or old, that captures a collective mind will have the power of buzz.

Our habit of adopting the ideas that surround us seems hard-wired into our brains, perhaps because a cooperative spirit gave our ancestors an evolutionary edge. We seem to have an antenna for buzz, and we often base our decisions on what we hear. In social psychology, our habit of looking to others for guidance is known as the heuristic of *social proof*. Social proof is one of the most powerful of heuristics: we so often take our cue of what to say and do from what we see others saying and doing that we may not notice its influence. If you're in an audience, and everyone stands up for an ovation, chances are you'll stand too—no matter what you thought of the show. If you know nothing more about an issue than that 95 percent of all Americans are for it, you'll be favorably inclined toward it before you even hear what it is. And if everyone is talking about an idea, you'll probably assume it's worth talking about.

Tom Harrison admits that even after twenty years in the public relations business, he's still taken by surprise when he unexpectedly uncovers the power of buzz. Tom tells the story of a client of theirs, a large, international relief organization, that for twenty years had run television ads asking for donations to aid people in third-world countries. Tom's agency tracked the giving and had a database that revealed a pattern of donation over all that time, which seemed infallible at predicting future levels. "If it's Syracuse, and they're calling at nine at night," Tom told me, "we know how much they'll really give. If it's Chicago, and it's six in the morning or three o'clock in the afternoon, they'll say, 'I'll give you twenty dollars a month.' We know what they'll really do over time."

But when famine struck Ethiopia, the television news coverage drove calls to the relief organization beyond all records, and viewers pledged more than they ever had before. When it came time to send in their money, though, an astonishing thing happened: A huge number of donors reneged on their pledges.

Nothing in the database predicted this. To find out what happened, the company held focus groups of delinquent donors in two cities and asked questions based on what they thought had caused the problem. They asked donors if they thought that the money wasn't getting through to the people who needed it. The answer was no. They asked if the donors thought the famine was over. The answer was no. They asked if the donors thought the organization was corrupt. The answer was no.

The experts had run out of questions. Tom remembers finally saying:

"Okay, we give up. Why didn't you give?" It was unanimous. They all said things like, "Tom Brokaw stopped talking about it." "It's not on the front page of the newspaper anymore." One guy even went so far as to suggest that we only raise money for things that are in the news media.

In short, the buzz was ebbing. Although people still believed in the need, the lack of media coverage was their cue to move that idea down in their list of priorities for belief or action.

Dying buzz can end a business project just as surely, but there are other, more subtle examples of buzz in action (and nonaction) in the workplace. When most people in a meeting agree, we feel a pull to go along. If we spot a company policy that's long-standing but seems unproductive, we're hesitant to challenge what everybody is already doing. The influence of the group is what can drive some ideas forward and kill others forever, so judging the buzz of ideas and projects at work is essential.

In this section we'll look at how buzz works and how you can use it to boost your messages, as well as what to do when the buzz is against you.

The Dynamics of Buzz

Trying to grasp the nature of buzz is like trying to describe every form of electricity. It's easy to see buzz in a fad flashing like a lightning bolt through America's teenagers; harder to recognize that buzz wires us together like the minute electrical charges that connect neurons into a single brain. The size and shape of buzz changes, but it always has certain qualities:

Buzz has a life cycle. Buzz goes through a cycle of birth, growth, maturity, and death. Buzz is born when people begin thinking along the same lines or react to an event in the same way: guitar players in Seattle are moved by a particular sound; conservative churchgoers enter politics in reaction to a liberal victory; visitors fall in love with Santa Fe, New Mexico; or you and a few coworkers envision a way to solve the shipping problem. As more people become interested in these new feelings and ideas, buzz grows.

On the brink of maturity, buzz gets a name. The name doesn't describe all the ideas in the buzz, which would be impossible, but the buzzword or phrase provides a way of referring to the buzz without going into a long explanation. That's when the Seattle sound becomes *grunge*, the *religious right* becomes a movement; *southwestern* means more than geography, or you decide to call your new shipping system *the quick-ship method*.

A buzz's biggest growth spurt begins just after it receives a name. As buzz matures, it collects appealing and popular concepts under its mantle and rids itself of marginal ideas until it represents a consensus of thought. This is the time when the name of the buzz has the most power. A financial executive told me about a current buzzword that appeals to investors:

In the investment community today, if you slap the word China or Pacific Rim or Asia development, or something like that, onto an endeavor that you're pursuing or stock that you're trying to sell, you'll have an enormous amount of success. You sell it as a China story: "This is a way to take advantage of the enormous growth potential of China." You're going to grab their attention right there. And you're going to attract capital that way. There are a lot of investment funds that have attracted billions of dollars that are just sitting in funds. People have put money in these funds, and these funds don't even have projects to invest in yet. But they've been able to attract all this money on the bet by investors that they're going to make a lot of money because somehow, some way this money's going to end up in China.

Once maturity has been reached, the buzz has plateaued. It may continue for years as part of our mental landscape, but its buzzword won't create the immediate flush of excitement it once did. The buzz becomes overcrowded, adopted by both sincere believers and obvious hucksters. Eventually, buzz dies, whether it lived for fifteen minutes or fifteen millennia (as did Ptolemy's earth-is-the-center-of-the-universe buzz).

The most visible buzz is new, but the most influential is old. People tend to assume that the latest thinking is an improvement over what came before, and so we pay more attention to new buzz, such as an emerging overseas market or a technological advance. But the great majority of our actions are based on buzz that's endured through the years: ideas such as the work ethic, free enterprise, and democracy. Because new buzz is both more enticing and malleable than old buzz, new buzz usually offers more opportunity for boosting communication.

Buzz travels in waves. Buzz usually starts in one place and travels to another, sometimes adding to its strength and sometimes leaving behind people who no longer care about it. In popular culture, the west and east coasts tend to develop buzzes in music, fashion, art and entertainment that travel toward the interior of the country. In many companies, the same sort of dynamic happens, with buzz being generated in headquarters, for example, and then traveling to the branches.

The ideas in buzz can be described, but not defined. Part of what makes buzz vibrate is the friction between different interpretations of what the buzz is really about. Take the long-standing buzz of environmentalism, for example. To claim yourself as an environmentalist, some people think you ought to recycle glass and aluminum; others think that nothing short of chaining yourself to a redwood will include you in the group. Buzz is public and personal at the same time. Underlying all buzz—even pragmatic ideas like total quality management—is a personal, emotional attachment that is, to a greater or lesser degree, irrational.

Buzz is composed of what people think and say, not necessarily of what they do. Buzz can be influential without being accurate. In her book *Backlash*, Susan Faludi describes how some of the backlash buzz about working women began with inaccurate trend stories in the media:

> The trend story is not always labeled as such, but certain characteristics give it away: an absence of factual evidence or hard numbers; a tendency to cite only three or four women, typically anonymously, to establish the trend; the use of vague qualifiers like "there is a sense that" or "more and more"; a reliance on the predictive future tense ("Increasingly, mothers will stay home to spend more time with their families"); and the invocation of "authorities" such as consumer researchers and psychologists, who often support their assertions by citing other media trend stories.

Business gets this treatment every time a new management style starts a buzz. How many people are actually using the new style is always impossible to know, but it's usually clear that many people have been influenced by it simply because they've heard of it, and it has a buzz.

Greater influence creates faster, stronger buzz. People are, of course, more likely to follow the lead of those who are like them or those who influence them. What is sometimes surprising is how much of a difference this can make.

A clear example of how this works in a social group comes from an experiment by animal behaviorists. The goal of the experiment was to get a group of monkeys to like a new food. Researchers found that when they gave the food to the monkeys with the lowest status, social proof did propel the taste for the candy through the group—but it took a year and a half, and even then only half were willing to eat it, a portion that didn't include any of the leaders. In another group, when they gave the dominant animals the new food, *all* the monkeys were happily eating it within *4 hours*.

Buzz that comes from an authoritative source (often called opinion leaders) will be stronger and will last longer than buzz that bubbles up from the rank and file. This doesn't mean that authority figures can *declare* buzz. We look to people we respect for buzz, not necessarily people who have power over us.

Conversely, if a buzz is among a number of diverse groups who don't have much influence over each other, the buzz won't last. I recall working on a strategic plan that my company's senior management, board of directors, and funders all agreed was top priority. Our committee was charged with drafting a document that would unify our effort to move the company from its stalled position. This buzz evaporated, though, once the first draft was completed. Each group realized that their differences couldn't be solved by one document. The buzz cooled, and the strategic plan was suddenly on the back burner, where it stayed, as far as I know, long after I had left the company.

Uncertainty increases the power of buzz. When people feel insecure, they instinctively look to others to decide what to think or do. The greater the insecurity, the more likely they will emulate someone else. This creates a kind of inertia in an uncertain group. It may be hard to get the first few people to accept an idea, but once they have, the chances are much greater that the rest will follow.

Uncertainty can increase the buzz of nonaction. There's a strange corollary hidden in the fact that uncertainty creates more pressure to conform: Since everybody is watching everybody else, if nobody knows what to do, nothing will be done. Psychologists call this the effect of *pluralistic ignorance*. Pluralistic ignorance is what causes witnesses to passively watch a horrible crime without trying to stop the criminal or even call the police. Everyone is uncertain of what to do, and when they look around, they see that no one else is doing anything.

You certainly have seen pluralistic ignorance in action in a meeting where no one seems to be able to make a decision, where everyone decides they need more information or that the decision should be passed to someone else or simply postponed. In other words, they decide not to decide.

These dynamics of buzz ripple through the communication in an office each day, boosting buzz here, cutting it there, and determining is small ways what people will believe and how they will behave tomorrow.

Tuning In

There are two ways to use buzz to boost your business communication. The first is to weave your message into a current buzz that is growing, or even one that has reached maturity, if that buzz still has power. The second, and more ambitious way, is to try to create a message that has potential for creating its own buzz. In either case you first must seek out and understand the various buzzes that surround you, analyzing the stories, news, rumor, and gossip you hear in the light of the dynamics of buzz described in the last chapter.

The most basic buzz to identify and understand is the collection of buzzes that ground a company: its corporate culture. These are the beliefs and values that, over the years, the majority of its people have come to accept as true. They may be specific beliefs, such as thinking that participation in a particular trade show or professional organization is essential, or that "the customer expects our brand to be inexpensive." But they may also be more general—conservative or aggressive business practices, for example.

Although its corporate culture is a company's most pervasive buzz, it's not always easy to *recognize* it as buzz; it's hard to see the forest for the trees. Like a tribe, a company learns through group experience; those lessons are codified in the stories that company veterans tell. Encouraging people to talk about the company's history—its founding, growth, mergers, failed products or ventures, successes, entries into new markets, restructures—will reveal the problems it had to deal with and the values it learned to rely upon to solve them.

The buzz of corporate culture is also recorded in company publications: annual reports, employee newsletters, press releases, brochures, and advertisements. No one sample is likely to tell the whole story; the more you can examine, the more accurate picture you'll have, like an archeologist unearthing the relics of an ancient civilization.

Companies may hold values in all kinds of realms, but four areas seem to be common to most companies:

Art vs. science. For some companies, the talent and good judgment of their people are considered the most fundamental truths; others never make a move without collecting as much quantifiable data as possible.

Expediency vs. care. Many corporations can only thrive if they beat deadlines, get to market first, or pack in as many jobs per hour as possible. For others, a single mistake can carry huge consequences, so the overriding value is caution.

Innovation vs. regulation. Coming up with solutions to a constant flow of new problems can be the main activity of some companies, while others provide consistent, dependable repetition of the same tasks or adherence to the letter of government contracts.

Independence vs. control. A company may allow plenty of latitude to its separate branches, representatives, departments and individuals, or it may try to tightly control them.

These values (and others) make up the buzz of corporate culture. It's old, powerful, and universal, which means it's unlikely to change except in glacial increments. That has three implications for communication: first, corporate culture isn't a dynamic enough buzz to propel a message; second, any buzz or message that conflicts with it has a slim chance of survival; and third, it is the buzz people will return to after a temporary fling with another buzz or in times of uncertainty.

The one exception to the influence of old corporate buzz is in a young, entrepreneurial company. If a company is young, so is its fundamental buzz, and because the company has nothing more to rest upon than this, then that buzz is strong enough to carry a message. It's the kind of buzz that originally helped carry Apple computers from a garage to the Fortune 500.

Overlying corporate culture are buzzes that are specific to each division, branch, or department of a company. This is a set of values that largely conforms to the corporate culture but that also deviates in a way that expresses a department's individuality.

Often, much of this buzz depends on the work of the division or department. An accounting department will probably have several values in common with accounting departments everywhere— values not necessarily embraced by the larger company. The same will be true of the advertising department, the research department, the sales department, and so on. But a particular department will also have its own history and beliefs, like a clan within the larger tribe. People who have worked in a department for a long time are a good source of this wisdom, especially if they've worked elsewhere in the company and can contrast different departments. Old memos and reports can also offer clues. Departmental buzz isn't as immutable as corporate culture, and it can sometimes be adapted to carry a message, especially if the department's manager has a particular vision. Departments often vie for influence over the company's corporate culture, tugging it one way or the other.

On top of the two layers of corporate culture and departmental culture run the buzzes that make up the fluid exchange of information inside a company. Some might last for a few months or even years, while others evaporate in a day or two. Some may be growing or about to crest, while others are petering out. Some might have potential to grow because they are building among a group of powerful people; others may be doomed for any number of reasons, although the people circulating them won't necessarily understand why when their buzz suddenly dies.

Sources for the Current Buzz

Finding current buzzes and analyzing them takes constant monitoring, a special kind of investigation, and regular communication with particular people.

Your supervisor. Finding the buzz behind company projects means looking for the deeper "why" behind an assignment. Supervisors are in the habit of instructing their staff to carry out duties with more or less explanation. By asking a few questions based on your best guesses, you can sometimes tease out clues to a buzz that's driving a project. Your boss may ask you to prepare information that will be passed on to someone higher up. What will it be used for? How does it fit into the larger strategy? Does your boss agree or disagree with the direction? These kinds of questions can reveal the shape of buzz that's forming somewhere in the higher levels of your company.

Secretaries. Forming an ongoing relationship with the secretaries and assistants of upper-level people is one of the best ways to find out what's on the minds of senior management. Secretaries are always concerned with what their bosses are thinking and often need someone to share their concerns with. Good secretaries won't betray the confidence of their bosses, but their bosses' general concerns, major projects, or recent meetings aren't usually confidential, although they might not be common knowledge, and can yield clues to the buzz that's commanding his or her attention.

Other departments. Anyone who has a view of the company from a different department, no matter what their position, can have information that helps fill out the full picture of buzz. Their information can often reveal a new buzz or can offer more detail about a buzz you may have unearthed elsewhere.

Industry news. Companies, of course, exist in and react to their environment. Outside sources such as suppliers, clients, customers, trade publications, and professional associations can often alert you to an event or circumstance that may be causing buzz inside your company.

Collecting Buzz

No matter where you gather buzz, it's important not to color the information you get. Don't begin a conversation with a leading phrase such as, "I hear everyone's talking about . . ." unless you need to show some of your knowledge to draw out your source. Generally, it's better to use open-ended questions such as, "What's going on?" or "What's keeping you busy?" or "What's your department (boss, staff) working on these days?" It's also important to *close* conversations with another open-ended question, because people will often leave information out of a conversation, thinking it's irrelevant or wouldn't be of interest to you. By asking one more time, "Anything else going on?" you cause your source to search for a last thing to say. Sometimes it's important.

Listening in on a conversation that's not directed at you, such as a talk in the hallway or around the coffee machine, can often give you pure buzz. If it seems appropriate, you can join in the conversation and learn more.

Pay attention to buzz that seems to have nothing to do with business—because it may suddenly become relevant in a way you can't foresee. It's doubtful that flannel shirt makers or workboot manufacturers thought much about MTV before the network propelled the grunge look into a mainstream buzz, creating new markets for those products. *Wired* magazine heralded the coming Internet mania long before it became de rigueur for a company to have a World Wide Web site.

Analyzing Buzz

Once located, buzz needs to be evaluated. When most people hear some news or gossip they'll usually try to decide how accurate it might be, but really assessing the usefulness of a particular buzz requires a more thorough look at the dynamics described in the last chapter.

Life cycle. You might hear buzz in any stage of its development. If you're new to a company and you learn of a major concern, you might assume that the information is new, too. In reality, it might be breathing its last, passed to you by someone who's not particularly astute or reading the writing on the wall. You also might be told that another buzz is "old news," although it might still be growing and have yet to reach its real influence. Like a reporter, you should have at least two reliable sources (and preferably more) before deciding how important a buzz is or is likely to be.

Timing is critical. Because buzz is perishable, only buzz that's growing or that seems to be in the early stages of a long life should be considered as something you might link your messages to. One signal that a buzz has reached critical mass is that it has just received a name—a buzzword—that hasn't yet been overused. In rare cases you may recognize that a buzz has become widespread but hasn't yet acquired a name. If you can create the name that's adopted, you'll have a particularly powerful influence on the direction it takes from that point on.

Judging the age, potential, and staying power of buzz is an art, not a science, and will also depend on your own belief about how good the actual content of the buzz is.

Consistency with older buzz. If a new buzz contradicts an old, powerful buzz, it has a peculiar attraction, especially for malcontents. That initial energy can fool you into thinking that change is in the air, that a new day is dawning, and that you would do well to link your message to it. The cases when this is true are, unfortunately, rare: Groups of people tend to resist change. Linking your message to the failed buzz of a group of rebels can taint your communication for a long time.

What's much more powerful and reliable is old buzz that's been made new. The idea of rugged individualism, for example, is a stable, old, all-American buzz that has been recycled again and again, most recently under the name of entrepreneurism. In a similar way, the computer department of a company may revive the old buzz of central control by introducing the "new" idea of networking individual computers together.

Origin. Knowing where a buzz came from can help you know where it's going and how long it will travel. When buzz is clearly from the higher levels in a company, that usually means it's a good candidate for carrying your message—but not always. Sometimes a direction can be declared by a director or vice-president whom other executives are aligned against. At other times, even the CEO can push a new idea and get lip service from senior management but no real commitment. The rule of confirming buzz from several different sources can help you know if buzz from above truly carries weight.

Buzz from other sources can have influence beyond what seems to be its face value. Look for ideas hatched by a powerful person's pet staffer or the new project from a department whose last project was a runaway success. Other sources are sometimes outside consultants (if we're paying for this advice, it must be valuable, and we will put it to work) and new employees (he or she is seen as bringing a "new perspective" that may be adopted for the same reason an outside consultant's will).

Content. One of the most difficult things to judge about a buzz is what ideas it actually contains and how people will interpret them. An example might be a tool manufacturer that for years has used advertising that compared their tools' features point-by-point with the competition. Let's assume a consumer survey reveals that the great majority of the company's customers buy its tools not because of a particular feature but because they have found that the tools last longer than others. A new buzz might then grow from the marketing department that is essentially "the sales story we should be telling in our advertising and through our reps is our reputation for durability." Different people in different departments might interpret this buzz in different ways. To the advertising department, this might suggest that their ads change from point-by-point feature comparisons to a more emotional appeal based on reputation. The sales reps, though, might continue to emphasize features but might shift to those that add to the tool's durability. They might agree with the buzz but think the ad department's interpretation is off the mark.

It's this quality of buzz—that the ideas are subject to interpretation—that makes it adaptable to new messages. When you first hear a buzz, you'll naturally interpret it according to your own view, as everybody else will. But to study and use buzz, you must try to collect and understand as many interpretations of a buzz as you can. This gives you more flexibility in fitting your message into a buzz.

The influence of uncertainty. When things are uncertain, the power of buzz increases. Sometimes that will mean a retreat to older ideas, the ones in a company's corporate culture, but it can also create a kind of panic that causes people to feel they need to jump on a bandwagon—any bandwagon. The buzz that seems so strong today may collapse tomorrow to be replaced by another new idea or by falling back on familiar values.

Before you sign on to a buzz by contributing your message, estimate how much, if any, of the enthusiasm people have for it comes from their own insecurity.

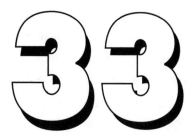

Linking to Buzz

After surveying the buzz in your environment, and analyzing it, you should now see the communications environment as a constantly changing buzz seascape, like an ocean filled with currents, prevailing winds, sudden squalls, and some calm seas. Navigating is a necessity; everyone must do that to survive. Using buzz to propel your messages, though, is like learning how to ride the currents and catch the favorable winds to move your ideas in the fastest possible way.

Linking a message to the buzz is something you've probably already done. You might have recognized that an idea of yours was complimentary to an idea that was already popular, thought about the connections, and expressed your idea in a way that emphasized some of the similarities.

Professional communicators in public relations or advertising *always* look for a way to link a message to a buzz (or at least how it will be seen in the light of current buzz), and they approach the task systematically. (They don't always succeed; if they can't find a buzz to link to, they'll craft a message meant to create its own buzz, which is covered in the next chapter.)

Although they are systematic and deliberate, professionals tend to develop their own intuitive process to find buzzlinks. Methods vary, but they often start with a brainstorming session with at least two people. They have learned that in the beginning, the quantity of ideas is more important than the quality of ideas, so they will toss out suggestion after suggestion, as many as they can think of and as fast as they can think of them, without much regard for their practicality. This usually leads to a lot of joking around, which I believe is a key part of the process. Humor is a by-product of the effort to make unusual connections. To create humor, you have to go outside the usual boundaries and find odd and absurd connections between ideas. Being in the frame of mind to see unusual connections is exactly what's needed to see the connections between your message and the buzz that might carry it.

Listening to the radio one day, I heard the newscaster announce that on a particular day Domino's Pizza had broken all records for home-delivered pizza in a single hour. That day was June 17, 1994; it was the day of the slow-speed chase of O. J. Simpson across the freeways of Los Angeles. That is an example of an unusual link: somebody working for Domino's had managed to discover a connection between their message—in this case, something like "Domino's Pizza is popular"—and the buzz of the hour, which was the murder trial of a famous sports star. Whether it was appropriate for Domino's to promote pizza this way is debatable, but the ingenuity of their buzzlink skills can't be faulted.

Increasing your skills at seeing the links you might make between your message and the prevailing buzz will take practice and a methodical approach that roughly follows what professionals do. If you can go through the process with the help a coworker, so much the better, although the method proposed here also works well if you're working alone. It's a two-part process.

Phase One: Brainstorming

In the first phase, your goal is to think of as many kinds of buzz and ways your message might be linked to those buzzes as possible. Your thinking should be the interaction of three things: your message, your audience, and the buzz. Each idea might start with any one of these components and then lead to the other two. For example, you might remember that there was a buzz you heard from one part of the company that consumers want products they can repair themselves. Next, look at your message. Let's say you have an idea for a product improvement and you want to find out what people think of your suggestion. You may see that the improvement would make do-it-yourself repair easier, which means you have found an exploitable link between the buzz and your message. Finally, imagine if this link would appeal to your audience. Retailers might not like the idea because they would make less money repairing products. Your company's customer representatives might not like it because they envision themselves on the phone for hours guiding consumers through the repairs. But senior management might subscribe to the buzz, and be willing to support your idea. If they are your target audience, then you have found an effective buzzlink.

Once you have one buzzlink, write it down and try to think of another. Keep going until you've exhausted either your capacity for new ideas or your time. These guidelines should help:

1. Use a blank pad of paper and a pen—not a computer. The manual approach helps enforce the rules of brainstorming: a pen instead of a pencil, to eliminate the temptation to erase and correct, and unlined paper instead of a keyboard, so you can sketch an idea when words fail you.

2. Move from words to pictures and back again. Seeing new connections often comes from bridging the natural divisions between the two hemispheres of the brain: the left, in charge of language and logic, and the right, in charge of pictures and feelings.

You might begin by thinking of some of the buzzes that you think might have something to do with your message. If these buzzes have a concise buzzword or short description, write it down. At this point, don't be afraid of writing down a buzz that on second thought you feel doesn't apply. In brainstorming, it's always better to get it on paper. If it doesn't work, it will be eliminated later.

If a buzz you are thinking of doesn't seem to have coalesced into a word or phrase, you can write down your own if one comes to mind. If not, try envisioning a process or circumstance in which the buzz might be expressed. You might see a meeting in which someone is presenting the essential ideas of the buzz by using charts and graphs. Sketch what these would look like. The buzz may involve a way of warehousing goods, which might mean the warehouse office would need to be laid out in a particular way. Draw a floor plan. The buzz you are thinking about might mean a different kind of advertising; sketch a magazine ad.

Picturing places, events, and things may in turn lead to new words, which you can then write down. Interplay between the realms of words and pictures is what often builds the connections that can link an idea to buzz.

3. Don't embellish. In brainstorming, quantity, not quality, counts. If you jot down a phrase or picture and feel it represents the essence of your idea but not the nuances, move on to your next idea. Time taken to come up with perfect wording or a neat diagram is wasted at this stage; that is done later once bad ideas have been eliminated.

Sometimes it's hard to know if you are embellishing or moving on to a new idea. There are no hard-and-fast rules—it comes with practice and judgment. From time to time look over your brainstorming sheets to assess how many ideas you've produced.

4. Don't try to conserve paper. Worrying about wasting paper leads to editing and trying to draw small or accurately.

Phase Two: Editing

When you have finished generating buzzlinks, the next phase is to edit what you have. It is important that you don't mix the two phases. Editing during the brainstorming phase will limit the number of ideas you have to choose from. Brainstorming during the editing phase means that you didn't really finish brainstorming and will also lead to a muddying of the two phases, which will cause a breakdown in the efficiency of the process.

Here are the editing steps:

1. Work by elimination, not by choice. You may go into the editing phase excited over one or two ideas and will want to develop them immediately. This defeats the purpose of the brainstorming, which was to develop many possibilities from which to choose. To avoid the problem, start editing by crossing out ideas that clearly won't work. You should have at least a few, including (I hope) some silly ideas you wrote down to make yourself laugh and loosen up. The first time you sort through your ideas don't deliberate long; if you can't decide immediately if an idea should be eliminated or not, then leave it in.

2. Weigh the merits. You are now left with ideas that have at least some merit. To sort through these, look again at the two connections within each buzzlink: your message's connection with the buzz and the buzz's connection with the audience. Looking at your list this way should help you cut out a few more possibilities: the ones in which your message would have to be distorted to fit with a buzz, and the ones you think rely on a buzz your audience isn't interested in. What you will have left are buzzlinks that have at least one strong connection within them.

3. Refine and develop. With the losers out of the way, you can now spend some time improving the buzzlinks you have left. Some won't need improvement; you can see that they accurately reflect your message and that their buzz would appeal to the audience. Others will have a weak link, but with a little thought these can sometimes be strengthened so that they become a viable option. You may also find that two buzzlinks may merge into one by eliminating the weak links and combining the strong ones.

4. Pick one. When you decide to commit to one, don't look back. Don't try to hedge your bets by including parts of the rejected buzzlinks, "just in case." The strongest buzzlinks are those that seem meant to be.

The Missing Link

It's not too unusual for all this effort to fail to produce a useful buzzlink, and it's a good idea to be prepared for this. If you begin the process assuming that you'll come out with a sure-fire way to promote your idea, you're liable to take what you get—and it may not be appropriate. In the end, you must stand back and judge whether the buzzlink you've created makes sense—for your message and for your audience. If it seems manipulative or insincere—in short, if the buzzlink seems more fabrication than fact—then you must abandon it. You and your message will be better served by taking the more difficult route of trying to create interest without a connection to any outside buzz.

Buzz from Zero

Starting buzz from scratch is difficult—ironically, because of the power of buzz itself. If you can't link your message to another buzz, that means the buzz you will try to generate will be competing against existing buzzes. Particularly troublesome are: old, established buzz, such as that in corporate culture; and pluralistic ignorance, which you'll recall is the tendency to avoid action if we see that no one else is acting.

In most cases, your message probably won't advocate values that oppose your company's corporate culture, although your idea might still be perceived that way. To avoid being accused of heresy, try to find ways to mention corporate values in your message and show how your idea reinforces them. This isn't usually too hard, because corporate values are general enough that they can include a broad range of ideas beneath their canopy.

If your message does fly in the face of the established norms, your only choice is to emphasize that and to ride on the friction that it will generate. It's a trial-by-fire strategy; one that may succeed if it attracts enough people who want to change the culture itself. The most useful hooks to help generate this kind of buzz are "It's New" and "It's Unavailable." Emphasizing the newness of your idea will attract attention, and telling people that your idea is something that the powers that be would rather not have revealed will help lend credibility to your suggestions. Two spins that would be helpful are "The Story" and "The Paradigm Shift." In your story, you would emphasize a David-and-Goliath drama, pitting your idea against the established way. You could also explain that your concept is a new way of thinking to which the old rules don't apply. Getting a firm commitment is particularly important for this kind of message; you need people to have an investment in your idea so they won't change their mind when the inevitable pressure mounts.

Pluralistic ignorance is a tougher problem. It is a universal force that, like gravity, brings everything to a halt unless there is enough energy to escape its pull. Most ideas die because people "lose interest," or "move on" or "get distracted," all euphemisms for sinking back into the comfort of procrastination and indecision that plagues most offices.

You have two tools to fight pluralistic ignorance. The first is to isolate people when you present an idea, so they are less likely to look elsewhere for what to do. The second is to custom-craft a message for each individual you approach, so you can ensure that it contains as many motivating hooks and spins as possible.

Your instinct to get the word out on your idea may be to communicate it to several people at once, either as a memo or e-mail or in a meeting. But this is not a good way to generate buzz. By launching a generic message to several people, you allow them to compare notes, to sound each other out. The rule of pluralistic ignorance predicts that people will be cautious and that *caution itself* will be communicated and grow as a buzz—a buzz that will deaden your idea.

Ideally, you should approach people one by one. An individual letter, memo, or e-mail lets you personalize your pitch, although it still allows your audience to get other opinions before responding to you. If it's possible, the best communication to spread buzz is personal conversation, either by phone or in person, in which you can both create a custom-made appeal and, most importantly, ask for a commitment.

Building buzz by approaching people one by one may seem tedious, but it is the most reliable way. Trying to increase a buzz too quickly will yield unpredictable results. "There are different reactions depending on the speed of integration," notes Scott Ray. "If you want an excited, frenzied, frenetic and uncontrollable and not necessarily predictable reaction, you can push it to the limit. You can just slam people with information and very often that will get them to do what you want. It may also get other things included in it that you don't want."

A plan to build buzz will benefit from following these guidelines:

Give your buzz a name before you start. As we saw earlier, at some point in the life cycle of buzz, it gets a name. If you're developing buzz from scratch, you should create a name *before* you present a buzz to your audience. This does two things: it allows people to pass on the information about the buzz easily, using the buzzword or phrase, and it makes it seem that the buzz is just reaching maturity, since it is a fully developed set of concepts, complete with a name.

A name also lets you customize a set of hooks and spins for a particular person and yet still assign these ideas one label. People will champion the label but will interpret the buzz in their own way. Your buzzphrase, the *quick-ship method,* may mean different things to different people, but the name lets everyone agree on a general direction.

Identify and convince opinion leaders. Buzz spreads faster when it is delivered by people of influence. Although this may mean convincing those who have official authority, it doesn't mean you need to rely entirely on top-down communication. In any organization, there are those who are listened to, who are known for their good judgment. Often, these people are the peers of those you want to influence.

Seek out and foster relationships with people that hold sway over others by knowing their concerns and by entering into reciprocal relationships with them. When you present your idea, ask outright for their support and help when you promote your idea. The buzz will then become theirs as well as yours and has a better chance of succeeding.

Let the buzz grow naturally. Trying to force buzz to grow by constantly proselytizing will work against your buzz. Remember that when someone adopts your idea, they will create their own reasons for believing in it—the idea will grow its own legs. If you're trying to spread buzz in an environment of complicated interests and entangling alliances, it's especially important to wait, watch, and make small adjustments as you go by continuing a dialogue with the opinion leaders.

Coordinate and present. Once your buzz has stabilized among opinion leaders, you may be able to recruit whole groups using coordinated presentations. In these situations, you present your ideas to an audience that is seeded with opinion leaders who already support your idea and who have been briefed on your presentation. Their job is to move the social proof heuristic of the group from one of pluralistic ignorance to active commitment. When you make a point, one of the opinion leaders may ask a question and then comment that he or she thinks your idea is sound. When the group is moving toward agreement, ask the uncommitted members specifically for their approval; remember that commitment in front of a group will cause people to maintain that commitment longer.

This technique can be used in groups as small as three or four people and also in much larger groups, although you will need more opinion leaders to turn a larger crowd. You can also arrange a similar effect by coordinating responses to a broadly distributed memo. You may send the memo to a dozen people and ask your committed opinion leaders to contact the recipients and encourage them to support your idea.

After your buzz has begun to grow, you can encourage others to adopt it not only by telling them the idea but by telling them how popular it is. It's a technique used by professionals in politics. When President Clinton was suffering a beating in the press, his press secretary David Gergen encouraged a new buzz by telling a reporter from the *Los Angeles Times* what "people were saying":

Despite the press coverage, Clinton's stock is rising now, Gergen argued, because people have developed a clearer sense of his capacity for the job and of where he wants to take the country. That in turn has enabled Clinton to gain credit for the economy's recent strong performance, he said.

"People are saying: 'At least he's trying to line up the country's problems and do something about them. I may not agree on a lot of what he is trying to do, but he is not in denial about the country's problems,' " Gergen said.

Bad Buzz

In July of 1994, engineers at Intel discovered that their Pentium chip had a bug in it: In certain very specific calculations, it divided incorrectly, throwing the answer off by a few decimal points. The company didn't announce the problem. Instead, Intel simply hoped no one would find out.

Unfortunately, somebody did: a mathematician named Dr. Nicely. Intel tried to placate Nicely and to sweep him under the rug, but by December the buzz had exploded. As the fallout spread and computer owners began to fret that their machines were mentally deficient, Intel doggedly insisted that the chip's flaw produced a problem so rare that a normal user would almost never be affected. IBM disagreed and withdrew its Pentium-based computers from the market.

Mortified, but still struggling as they fought an impossible battle against a toxic cloud of bad buzz, Intel made small concessions, but wanted to avoid offering free replacements to every Pentium chip owner. Meanwhile, they watched their stock value drop. The buzz even grew its own jokes. Wags said there should be a new sticker on computers built with the Pentium: "Intel inside—can't divide." In the end, the company was forced to replace the chip of any and every Pentium chip owner who wanted a new one. Overall, the debacle cost Intel $475 million.

As Intel found out, bad buzz can kill reputations, profits, and careers. But bad buzz can be managed if you understand the dynamics that drive it.

When Heuristics Turn Against You

The Intel case is a classic example of how the wrong decisions can engage heuristics that will negate a message. It hardly mattered how factual Intel's argument was (and there is good evidence that they were right—that the flaw would affect almost no one), because the emotions aroused by heuristics completely overwhelmed their message.

Here are the heuristics Intel inadvertently triggered:

Pluralistic ignorance. When Intel's officers first discovered the chip's flaw, they no doubt wondered what they should do about it (besides fixing it in later chips). Evidently, they looked to each other for advice, and the inertia of the group towards inaction suppressed any suggestion that they take action.

The drama of the story. When the news broke, Intel had the misfortune of having its role cast by circumstances. The focus immediately shifted from the problem with the chip to the David-and-Goliath drama of the world's largest computer-chip maker being brought to its knees by an obscure mathematician. The fact that he was named Nicely was too delicious an irony for any reporter to resist emphasizing. That, and the fact that Dr. Nicely was nice (he was not outraged but felt let down, according to published interviews), accentuated the enormity and facelessness of Intel.

Reciprocity. Like any manufacturer, Intel is in a reciprocal relationship with its customers. When the company refused to replace the flawed chips immediately, computer owners felt Intel was not returning the trust they had given it.

Social proof. The media latched on to the story and repeated it endlessly, not only in blow-by-blow news stories but in columns and "how-to" articles (such as "How to Tell If Your Pentium Chip Has the Bug"). Since so many people were talking about the problem, social proof constantly reinforced the perception that the chips were simply "bad."

Scarcity. By trying to downplay the details of the chip's failure, it seemed that Intel was hoarding information. That information (whether there was any or not) seemed all the more valuable because Intel didn't seem to want to release it. When IBM released a report that the chip's malfunction was much more common than Intel had admitted, it seemed all the more likely that Intel was hiding something.

Competition. When Intel did decide to replace the chip for the users that could prove they had a need, they created what I have described earlier as a feeding frenzy: a competition for something scarce. That had the effect of only increasing the desire Pentium owners had of wanting a new chip.

Intel could have diffused much of the power of these heuristics if they had constructed their communication using other heuristics:

Joining their audience. When Intel first discovered the flaw, they had the opportunity to show that Intel and its audience had the same concerns. Had Intel immediately announced that they did not want a single user to have a problem and so would offer free replacements immediately, bad buzz would never have begun. They had the chance again when Dr. Nicely announced his discovery. Instead of seeming to set themselves against Nicely, they could have thanked him and perhaps even asked him to test their new chips, which would have also shown that they had their customers' concerns at heart.

Reciprocal concessions. Intel's posture seemed to be one of constant resistance, which violates the desire people have for reciprocity. The company could have reversed that impression by conceding on some points earlier. They had plenty of opportunities: They could have announced the problem themselves; they could have offered free chips when Dr. Nicely discovered the problem; they could have agreed with IBM when it released its devastating estimate.

Perceptual contrast. Intel tried to use this heuristic with their estimate that the flaw would affect the average user only once in 27,000 years, a figure that attempted to put the problem in perspective. The tactic didn't work because Intel had little credibility left due to its other mistakes. If this estimate had been announced immediately after a concession, it may have been more readily accepted.

Countering Bad Buzz

Once bad buzz has begun, there is a standard process public relations professionals use to solve it. Tom Harrison, a public relations executive, told me about a case he handled. His client, a major medical facility I'll call Friendwood Medical Center, was vandalized by animal rights activists, who videotaped the institution's alleged inhumane labs and alerted the National Institutes of Health (NIH) and the Food and Drug Administration (FDA). The NIH immediately pulled millions of dollars worth of funding, and the FDA launched an investigation into animal treatment at the facility, all of which was reported in the press.

Tom described his meeting with the board of directors:

I'll never forget this meeting. A bunch of angry people before I even started. And I said, "Now are we all clear on the fact that we're guilty?" I had people shouting at me and at each other, and I just sat there as calmly as possible and I said, "We can't even go on to the next point until everybody here understands we're guilty." And they're saying, "But we're Friendwood!, we're Friendwood!" Finally somebody was smart enough to say, "What are we guilty of?" And I said, "That's the key."

He went on to detail the minor code infractions of their laboratory, such as non-mold-resistant ceiling tile and narrow corridors—all easy to fix. He went on to explain the four fundamental steps of dealing with bad buzz that the hospital would have to employ:

1. Admit your fault. This first, essential step is the hardest for most people to accept. If you've been unjustly accused, admitting some culpability seems to be a step backwards. But the rule of reciprocal concessions demands that you find some point to give in on. Remember that reciprocal concessions depend more on the give-and-take aspect than on the actual content of what it is you are giving or taking, which means that you have some latitude in what you admit to. Once the admission is made, you have some credibility, which you will use to move to the next step.

2. Offer your explanation. Now that you've admitted guilt, your audience will feel you have earned the right to present your side of the story. This is where you should explain as fully as possible your actions and to use any spin you can to demonstrate that the charges against you are exaggerated.

3. Offer your remedy. Once you have defined the problem on your terms, you can define the solution you offer that will meet those terms. The more specific the better, although even to say you are launching a "thorough review of the situation" will help. If you can't fix the problem, tell why you're taking steps to make sure it never happens again.

4. Move to another subject. Change the subject and close the issue. It is like saying "That is behind us now—we know what will be done; let's focus on the future." If it seems appropriate, talk about something good that you'll be doing in the future, thereby turning the buzz from bad to good.

Friendwood followed this plan it its dealings with the press after the initial bad publicity. Yes, they said, they were guilty of some minor violations; however, the accusations of the animal activists were wrong: At no time were animals ever abused. They went on to announce the corrections they would make to solve the code infractions and estimated that the work would be completed in a matter of months. Finally, they closed with the message that the incident had not affected the confidence people had with the hospital, citing funding they received for a study that only five hospitals in the nation received. The buzz turned overnight. "They got overwhelming positive coverage on the study," Tom told me.

"Phones rang off the hook with people trying to get in. They filled a wing of the hospital."

The four steps that Friendwood used to diffuse bad buzz work on any scale, whether for a company, a department, or an individual.

AFTERWORD

Like any art, communication relies on a mixture of skills and talent that is hard to describe and impossible to define, which is why the techniques of Hook Spin Buzz can't be reduced to a simple formula for success. I'm reminded of the trouble another author had in explaining how to get the best results. In her cookbook *Love and Knishes* (Vanguard Press), Sara Kasdan tells of trying to capture her mother's art of making lokchen (noodles).

"Mama, you make the lokchen. I'll watch. But everything must be measured."

So good already. No. While she is measuring the flour the phone rings. When I come back from the phone she tells me, "I put in two and a half cups flour, but I see already it's too much."

I empty the flour from the bowl.

"What are you doing with my flour?" screams Mama.

"It's too much you say. So I'm putting back we should measure again."

"But I took out already a little with the hand. Now is right."

So it is with Hook Spin Buzz. Success depends on the quality of your ideas and your judgment; but even more, it depends on your personal style. These techniques trigger our emotions, and emotions are personal. If you don't know your own likes and dislikes, you can't expect to move others with your convictions. Trying to use every technique described here would be like trying to make every recipe in a cookbook. You shouldn't feel compelled to use any particular hook, spin, or buzz if it doesn't naturally appeal to you. If you don't like noodles, don't follow a recipe for lokchen.

Throughout the book, I have suggested ways to build into your messages heuristics that will help convince your audience to pay attention, see your point of view, and believe what you say. Follow the systems, learn the tools, and you will develop your skill. Experience will help you know which heuristic appeals will work best in a given situation, but your instinct will tell you when you've gone too far. Start with an "It's New" hook, increase the appeal with an "It's Unavailable" hook, add a "Give In to Win" spin, shift the paradigm, tell a story, add a "Sudden Twist," and work hard to create your buzz—then take out a little with the hand until it's right.

NOTES

Prologue: How This Book Will Improve Your Communication

3 Most of us realize that we humans use more than cool reason to make our decisions. The research, case studies, and theories that shed light on how this peripheral route of decision-making works have been neatly summarized in two books from which I've drawn my understanding: Anthony Pratkanis and Elliot Aronson's Age of Propaganda: *The Everyday Use and Abuse of Persuasion* (New York: W. H. Freeman and Company, 1992) and Robert B. Cialdini's *Influence: Science and Practice*, 3rd ed. (HarperCollins College Publishers, 1993).

A new theory is showing an even more intriguing link between emotion and decisions. In his book *Descartes' Error: Emotion, Reason, and the Human Brain* (New York: Grosset/ Putnam, 1994), neurologist Antonio R. Damasio argues that rationality requires emotion to function. He documents several patients who, through injury or disease, lost their ability for emotional response and with it the ability to make any kind of reasonable choices. Damasio also reveals that our common assumption that emotion is a "lower" function of the brain is wrong (p. 128):

> So blatant is the discrepancy between the processing capacities of "low and old" and "high and new" brain structures that it has fostered an implicit and seemingly sensible view on the respective responsibilities of those brain sectors. In simple terms: The old brain core handles basic biological regulation down in the basement, while up above the neocortex deliberates with wisdom and subtlety. Upstairs in the cortex there is reason and will power, while downstairs in the subcortex there is emotion and all that weak, fleshy stuff.
>
> This view, however, does not capture the neural arrangement that underlies rational decision-making as I see it. . . . The apparatus of rationality, traditionally presumed to be *neo*cortical, does not seem to work without that of biological regulation, traditionally pre-

sumed to be *sub*cortical. Nature appears to have built the apparatus of rationality not just on top of the apparatus of biological regulation but also *from* it and *with* it. The mechanisms for behavior beyond drives and instincts use, I believe, both the upstairs and the downstairs: The neocortex becomes engaged *along with* the older brain core, and rationality results from the concerted activity.

4 Cialdini, p. 8.

4 Business communicators are unaware of the power of heuristics because business texts and popular books teach communication using a completely different model. It's what I call the "radio analogy," in which there is a *sender* (someone or something that creates a signal);, a *signal* (the information to be communicated); an encoder, a *channel*, a *decoder*, a *receiver*, and *noise* (something that degrades or interrupts the signal). Variations of this theory appear in several books, including Tony Alessandra and Phil Hunsaker, *Communicating at Work* (New York: Fireside, 1993); Carl R. Anderson, *Management: Skills, Functions, and Organization Performance* (Dubuque, Iowa: Wm. C. Brown Publishers, 1984); Samuel C. Certo, *Principles of Modern Management*, 2nd ed. (Dubuque, Iowa: Wm. C. Brown Publishers, 1983); Richard M. Steers, *Introduction to Organizational Behavior*, 4th ed. (New York: HarperCollins, 1991); Andrew D. Szilagyi, Jr., *Management and Performance*, 2nd ed. (Glenview, Illinois: Scott, Foresman and Company, 1984) and many others.

This model tries to improve communication by focusing on correcting "errors." For example, if your boss turns down your proposal, the model might suggest you have committed an "encoding error" (you used language that was too technical) or that "noise" (a distracting phone call) degraded your "signal." In my view, the model isn't helpful because it characterizes "senders" and "receivers" as hardware devices instead of thinking, feeling people.

A human listener tunes in not just because a signal is clear or strong, but because its content is helpful or important. The idea of "encoding" and "decoding" presupposes there is only one way to interpret a message, when we know that different people will always have different reactions. Moreover, we know that a "channel" isn't an inert carrier of information; there's a big difference between meeting someone face-to-face and sending them a form letter.

Finally, the model ignores the fact that in humans, the content of a signal influences whether a channel stays open or shuts down. A radio, once it's tuned in, will sit happily receiving whatever comes over the air. A person won't.

1 Know Your Audience

11 My insistence on knowing your audience is based on the fact that public relations, advertising, and marketing professionals have found this to be the single most important step in trying to communicate a persuasive message—so they try to find out all they can. For example, Philip Kotler and Eduardo L. Roberto outline the information a researcher should gather in their book *Social Marketing: Strategies for Changing Public Behavior* (The Free Press, 1989), p. 27:

1. sociodemographic characteristics (external attributes of social class, income, education, age, family size, and so forth),
2. psychological profile (internal attributes, such as attitudes, values, motivation, and personality), and
3. behavior characteristics (patterns of behavior, buying habits, and decision-making characteristics).

Michael Weiss, in his book *The Clustering of America*, (New York: Perennial Library, 1988), pp. 206–9, shows how a thorough knowledge of an audience can be used to craft hooks for specific groups. Weiss describes the 1983 Louisiana gubernatorial campaign between incumbent David Treen and challenger Edwin Edwards. Polls showed the candidates even, but that a good portion of the population was undecided. Edwards' research revealed that the swing vote resided in three different groups, with three different sets of concerns. Consequently, his campaign sent out three different brochures.

To the financially conscientious middle class, the headline read "$1.7 Billion. And what have we got to show for it?"—an attack on the inflated budget of the Treen administration. To the normally apathetic voters in the poorer blue-collar group, the headline asked and answered the question: "Edwin Edwards.

David Treen. Does it really make a difference? You bet it does." The text stressed jobs, education, and finance. Residents of a small-town rural group got a headline designed to appeal to their longing for security: "It seems like so long ago," it began, "when we could walk down our own streets and feel safe. When we could pass the unemployment office and not see a line. When we were prospering." By knowing his audiences and using different hooks for each one, Edwards got his message across. He won by a landslide.

12 Sending the right signals: For an excellent and detailed description of the importance of nonverbal signals in communication and a guide to their use, see Robert Bolton, *People Skills* (New York: Touchstone, 1979) pp. 33–38.

12 Don't load questions: Marketing researchers know the response to a question can only be as good as the question itself. Wright, Warner, Winter, and Zeigler write in *Advertising*, 4th ed., (New York: McGraw-Hill, 1977), p. 538: "Leading researchers claim the greatest errors in survey results are due to the wording of questions." David Ogilvy notes how tough it is to put yourself in the place of someone you survey: "Waiting for a train in Pennsylvania station one evening, I was accosted by an interviewer and asked questions which I had written two days before. They were impossible to answer. I went back to my office and canceled the survey." (David Ogilvy, *Ogilvy on Advertising* [New York: Crown, 1983], p. 164.)

Questions in marketing surveys are either "closed," with a limited number of responses (Did you vote in the last election?) or "open," allowing for explanation (Why did you vote for the candidate you chose in the last election?). Pollsters use closed questions much more often, not because they offer better data but because the answers are more easily quantified. Open questions will always elicit more information, which is why I suggest using them, also suggested by Bolton, p. 44–45.

14 "Since women seek to build rapport . . ." Deborah Tannen, *You Just Don't Understand: Women and Men in Conversation* (New York: William Morrow, 1990), p. 125.

17 Seven kinds of intelligence: Howard Gardner, *Frames of Mind: The Theory of Multiple Intelligences*, (New York: Basic Books, 1983).

18 Weather reporters blamed for floods or droughts: David L. Langford, "Weathermen Pay Price for Nature's Curve Balls," *The Arizona Republic* (from The Associated Press), Dec. 18, 1981.

19 Experiment demonstrating that serving food increases acceptance of political statements: G. H. S. Razran, "Conditional responses changes in rating and appraising socio-political slogans," *Psychological Bulletin*, 37 (1940), 481.

2 Don't Sell Your Seed, Sell Their Lawn

21 "All politics is local": Tip O'Neill, quoted by Christopher Matthews, *Hardball* (New York: Summit Books, 1988, p. 44.)

21 Story about Congressman William J. Hughes: Matthews, pp. 45–46.

22 "I have seen one mail order advertisement . . .": John Caples, *Tested Advertising Methods* (New York: Prentice-Hall, 1974), p. 11.

23 "I'm not saying that charming, witty and warm copy . . .": Rosser Reeves, *Reality in Advertising* (New York: Alfred A. Knopf, Inc., 1961) quoted by David Ogilvy, *Ogilvy on Advertising* (New York: Crown, 1983), p. 24.

23 For an example of how the Unique Selling Proposition is used in advertising, see Wright, Warner, Winter, and Zeigler, pp. 409–411.

24 "Advertising which promises no benefit . . .": Ogilvy, p. 160.

25 Reeves summation of a USP: Reeves, p. 46.

3 To Receive, Give

27 Experiment with gift of soda and raffle tickets: Dennis Regan, "Effects of a favor and liking on compliance," *Journal of Experimental Social Psychology*, 7 (1971), 627–639.

28 Senator Robert Byrd sharpening pencils: Matthews, p. 54.

28 Story of Jerry Brown helping Sally Kellerman move: Cialdini, p. 26.

29 To Give, Receive: This is a truth known by politicians and is described by Matthews in his chapter entitled "It's Better to Receive Than to Give," pp. 59–73.

4 Use a Lead

32 I've borrowed the term *lead* from journalism. The *Random House Dictionary*, unabridged, 2nd ed. (New York: Random House, 1987), defines a journalistic lead as "A short summary serving as an introduction to a news story, article, or other copy." But to a journalist, it's much more than just a summary—it's what must keep the reader reading. Journalistic leads can be used in business writing; for an excellent guide to writing journalistic leads, see André Fontaine and William A. Glavin, Jr. *The Art of Writing Nonfiction*, 2nd ed. (Syracuse, New York: Syracuse University Press, 1987), pp. 118–126.

34 The term or idea of a handle is used by people in a number of professions where it's essential to sell a concept quickly. Michael Larsen uses the phrase *selling handle* in his book *How to Write a Book Proposal* (Cincinnati: Writer's Digest Books, 1985), pp. 22–24, and points out that a good handle continues to sell itself: "Your book passes through many hands on the road from writer to reader: agent, editor, salespeople, and booksellers. They all need a one-line sales-oriented handle to sell it to the next link in the publishing chain." Combining two ideas to create a handle is common in the book business; Larsen gives the example of pitching a book as "a French version of *Roots*." Movie people are also well-known for creating handles with combinations. Cynthia Whitcomb in her book *Selling Your Screenplay* (New York: Crown, 1988), p. 98, notes how some successful movies were pitched with combo handles: " '*High Noon* in outer space' (*Outland*); '*Summer of '42* with cars' (*American Graffiti*); '*Romeo and Juliet* on drugs' (*Panic in Needle Park*)."

35 Lloyd Bentsen on Dan Quayle: quoted by Cathleen Decker, "Clinton, Gore Invoke Imagery of the Kennedys," *Los Angeles Times*, July 20, 1992, Home Edition, sec. A, p. 1.

36 "By the skin of our teeth . . .": Barry Diller, "Don't Repackage—Redefine!" *Wired* magazine, 3.02 (Feb. 1995), p. 82, (transcript of his keynote address delivered at the American Magazine Conference in Laguna Niguel, California).

5 Make It Their Idea

37 Experiment with boys and toys: Jonathan Freedman, "Long-term behavioral effects of cognitive dissonance," *Journal of Experimental Social Psychology*, 1 (1966), 145–155.

39 Research on bargaining techniques: A. A. Benton, H. H. Kelley, and B. Liebling, "Effects of extremity of offers and concession rate on the outcomes of bargaining," *Journal of Personality and Social Psychology*, 24 (1972), 73–83.

40 Changing existing behavior patterns vs. creating new behavior patterns: Kotler and Roberto note on pp. 10–11: "Commercial advertising is effective because its task is not to instill basic new attitudes or create new behavior patterns but to channel existing attitudes and behavior in one direction or another. For example, a toothpaste manufacturer does not have to convince people to brush their teeth but only to direct them to use a particular brand of toothpaste. Preexisting attitudes are easier to reinforce than to change."

6 It's New!

44 Advertisements with news recalled by 22 percent more people: Ogilvy, p. 71.

44 "They should be boiled in oil": Ogilvy, p. 109.

45 Key principle in finding news is to look for a difference: The idea of looking for a difference to find news was developed in a personal conversation with Scott Ray, 1995.

7 It's Free!

47 For more on the influence of getting something for free, see Cialdini, pp. 26–29.

9 It's Unavailable!

51 Experiment of selling beef to supermarkets: A. Knishinsky, *"The effects of scarcity of material and exclusivity of information on industrial buyer perceived risk in provoking a purchase decision."* Doctoral dissertation, Arizona State University, Tempe, quoted by Cialdini, p. 208.

52 Speech against coed dorms: S. Worchel, S. E. Arnold, and M. Baker, "The effect of censorship on attitude change: The influence of censor and communicator characteristics," *Journal of Applied Social Psychology*, 5 (1975), 222–239.

52 Mock trials: D. Broeder, "The University of Chicago jury project," *Nebraska Law Review*, 38 (1959), 744–760.

54 Phantom choice: For a detailed description of how phantom choices influence decisions, see Pratkanis and Aronson, pp. 188–195.

10 Don't Lose Out

57 Breast cancer brochure: Reported by Cialdini, p. 196, from B. E. Meyerwitz, D. K. Wilson, and S. Chaiken, *"Loss-framed messages increase breast self-examination for women who perceive risk."* Paper presented at the meeting of the American Psychological Society, Washington, D.C., 1991.

12 What Your Package Says

62 The beautiful baby joke: Joseph Telushkin, *Jewish Humor* (New York: William Morrow, 1992), p. 56.

62 Experiment with MasterCard logo: Richard A. Feinberg, "Credit cards as spending facilitating stimuli," *Journal of Consumer Research*, 13 (1986), 348–356.

63–67 First impressions: Much of the information here is adapted from my book, *Looking Good on Paper* (New York: AMACOM, 1995), pp. 13–20.

Part II The Spin: A Fresh Perspective

73 Copy machine experiment: E. J. Langer, A. Blank, and B. Chanowitz, "The mindlessness of ostensibly thoughtful action: The role of 'placebic' information in interpersonal interaction," *Journal of Personality and Social Psychology*, 36 (1978), 635–642.

74 Aristotle's definition of rhetoric: Richard E. Hughes and P. Albert Duhamel, *Rhetoric: Principles and Usage* (Englewood Cliffs, New Jersey: Prentice-Hall, Inc., 1962), p. 4.

74 Spin's two steps: My ideas about the workings of spin come in part from Christopher Matthews. In the chapter entitled "Spin!" in his book he writes, "The dance was a traditional two-step: first, admit you have a problem, thereby establishing credibility; then use the enhanced credibility to define the problem in a way that keeps the political damage to a minimum," (pp. 177–178), and "The joy of spin lies in telling the accuser he is dead right and then getting the personal satisfaction of delineating exactly what he is right about," (p. 180).

14 Join Your Audience

77 Coin toss experiment: Described by Pratkanis and Aronson, pp. 167–168, referring to H. Tajfel, *Human Groups and Social Categories* (Cambridge, UK: Cambridge University Press, 1987).

77 Flashing faces experiment: R. F. Bornstein, D. R. Leone, and D. J. Galley, "The generalizability of subliminal mere exposure effects," *Journal of Personality and Social Psychology*, 53 (1987), 1070–1079.

78 Asking strangers for money: T. Emswiller, K. Deaux, and J. E. Willits, "Similarity, sex, and requests for small favors," *Journal of Applied Social Psychology*, 1 (1971), 284–291.

15 Boost Your Authority

84 Electrical shock experiment: Described by Cialdini, pp. 171–176, referring to S. Milgram, *Obedience to Authority* (New York: Harper & Row, 1974).

17 Give In to Win

98 Reciprocal concessions: A term used by Cialdini, p. 34.
99 "Always concede on principle": Matthews, p. 144.
99 "When sitting down to a deal . . .": Matthews, p. 152.
99 "Rejection-then-retreat": Cialdini, pp. 36–39.

18 Get a Commitment

102 Safe driving sign and billboard: J. L. Freedman and S. C. Fraser, "Compliance without pressure: The foot-in-the-door technique," *Journal of Personality and Social Psychology*, 4 (1966), 195–203.

102 "Grow legs": A term used by Cialdini, p. 80.

20 Spin on the Phone

112 Voice mail court case: Ben Dobbin, Associated Press, *Los Angeles Times*, Orange County Edition, Jan. 25, 1995, sec. D, p. 7.

21 Spin on Paper

115–119 Much of the material in this chapter is adapted from my book, *Looking Good on Paper* (New York: AMACOM, 1995).

119 Experiment with college students and cards: W. F. Dukes and W. Bavan, "Accentuation and response variability in the perception of personally relevant objects," *Journal of Personality*, 20 (1952), 457–465.

22 Spin on E-Mail

120–121 Bill Gates's E-mail figures and quotes: Amy Harmon, "The Cutting Edge; Mailbox Runneth Over? You Must Be Using E-Mail," *Los Angeles Times*, April 11, 1994, Home Edition, sec. D, pp. 2–11.

122 Macworld survey: Jonathan Weber, "No, Your Boss Doesn't Have Eyes in the Back of His Head; But There's a Good Chance He's Reading Your Private E-Mail," *Los Angeles Times*, May 22, 1993, Home Edition, sec. D, p. 1.

122 E-mail lawsuits: Leslie Helm, "The Digital Smoking Gun; Mismanaged E-Mail Poses Serious Risks, Experts Warn," *Los Angeles Times*, June 16, 1994, Home Edition, sec. D, p. 1.

23 Presentation Spin

123 "Facts push other facts . . ." Neil Postman, *Amusing Ourselves to Death, Public Discourse in the Age of Show Business* (New York: Penguin, 1985), p. 70.

24 Original Spin: The Story

126–127 Basic principles of drama: Aristotle laid down the fundamentals in *Poetics*; my understanding of drama has also been enhanced by Lajos Egri, *The Art of Dramatic Writing* (New York: Simon & Schuster, 1946); Robie Macauley and George Lanning, *Technique in Fiction*, 2nd ed., rev. (New York: St. Martin's Press, 1987); and Ben Brady and Lance Lee, *The Understructure of Writing for Film and Television* (Austin, Texas: University of Texas Press, 1988), among others.

127 "... consider the news story ..." James A. Autry, *Love & Profit; The Art of Caring Leadership* (New York: William Morrow, 1991), pp. 27–28.

129 A story's ability to induce experience without resistance: from a personal conversation with Scott Ray, 1995.

129 The "What," "So what," and "Now what," structure: A phrase Tom Harrison introduced to me in a personal conversation, 1995.

131 Ronald Reagan and David Stockman: Matthews, pp. 176–180.

131 Intel's problems with the Pentium chip: "Intel Takes $475-Million Earnings Hit," Jan. 18, 1995, *Los Angeles Times*, Home Edition, sec. D, p. 1.

131 dBase II: Peter Hay, *The Book of Business Anecdotes* (New York: Facts on File, 1988), p. 122–123.

25 Put on a Label

133 Congressman John Kaish "pleaded with reporters ...": George J. Church, *Time* magazine, May 22, 1995, p. 32.

134 Labels define how we think: I don't mean by this that we can only think in words. Steven Pinker in *The Language Instinct* (New York: HarperCollins, 1994) makes a convincing case against this idea (pp. 56–58):

In much of our social and political discourse, people simply assume that words determine thoughts. Inspired by Orwell's essay "Politics and the English Language," pundits accuse governments of manipulating our minds with euphemisms like pacification (bombing), revenue enhancement (taxes), and nonretention (firing) . . . [But] the idea that thought is the same thing as language is an example of what can be called a conventional absurdity: a statement that goes against all common sense but that everyone believes because they dimly recall having heard it somewhere and because it is so pregnant with implications. . . . Think about it. We have all had the experience of uttering or writing a sentence, then stopping and realizing that it wasn't exactly what we meant to say. To have that feeling, there has to be a "what we meant to say" that is different from what we said. Sometimes it is not easy to find *any* words that properly convey a thought. When we hear or read, we usually remember the gist, not the exact words, so there has to be such a thing as a gist that is not the same as a bunch of words. And if thoughts depended on words, how could a new word ever be coined? How could a child learn a word to begin with? How could translation from one language to another be possible?

What Pinker doesn't deny, and what is my point here, is that words still carry a great influence over our thoughts and actions.

134 Nuclear Magnetic Resonance scanner: Personal interview with Tom Harrison, 1995.

134 Volunteer Recruitment department: Personal interview with Tom Harrison, 1995.

135 Future Shock: Alvin Toffler's phrase and book title, *Future Shock* (New York: Bantam, 1970) is a label that has now worked its way into our language. The *Random House Dictionary* (2nd ed., unabridged, 1983), defines future shock as "physical and psychological disturbance caused by a person's inability to cope with very rapid social and technological change," or "any overload of a person's or an organization's capacity for adaptation or decision making [on the model of culture shock; popularized by a book of the same title (1970) by Alvin Toffler (b. 1928), U.S. journalist]."

26 Make a Metaphor

140–141 "Look at all the cracks around that door!": Pratkanis and Aronson, p. 128.

27 Shift the Paradigm

143 Although many books describe paradigm change, one of the best remains Thomas S. Kuhn's *The Structure of Scientific*

Revolutions, 2nd ed. (Chicago: The University of Chicago Press, 1970). Kuhn shows that even in the rational world of science a paradigm shift can overwhelm and invalidate existing rules to create new criteria for truth.

144–145 "You're not visiting an employer . . .": Richard Nelson Bolles, *What Color Is Your Parachute?* (Berkeley, California: Ten Speed Press, 20th anniversary ed., 1990), p. 162.

28 Use Numbers

148 The "shocking" and "alarming" statistics I created here about America's math ability were inspired by what Richard P. Runyon calls "WOW statements" in his book *How Numbers Lie* (Lexington, Massachusetts: The Lewis Publishing Company, 1981), p. 110.

150 Intel and IBM estimates of Pentium's failure: From the reports, it's actually difficult to figure out how either Intel or IBM came up with their estimates of the occurrence of the Pentium flaw. John Thompson, a spokesman for Intel, was quoted as saying "The average user is not going to see this thing, except maybe once in 27,000 years." (Martha Groves, "Mathematician Finds Intel's Pentium Doesn't Compute," *Los Angeles Times*, Nov. 24, 1994, Home Edition, sec. D, p. 1). A few weeks later, another article in the *Los Angeles Times* stated, "Intel has said a typical computer user using a spreadsheet and doing 1,000 divisions per day would notice a problem from the Pentium bug just once in 27,000 years. In its tests, however, IBM found that common spreadsheet programs, recalculating for 15 minutes a day, could produce errors as often as every 24 days." (Martha Groves, "IBM Stops Shipping Pentium PCs," *Los Angeles Times*, Dec. 13, 1994, Home Edition, sec. D, p. 1). In another article (Richard O'Reilly, "Does Your PC Have the Pentium Bug?" *Los Angeles Times*, Dec. 13, 1994, Home Edition, sec. D, p. 3), the specifics became even more puzzling:

Intel says only one in 9 billion sets of randomly generated numbers could be expected to trigger the error, and thus the average computer user is likely to encounter it only once in 27,000 years.

But IBM did its own probability analysis and concluded that a more likely error rate is once in every

100 million division operations. IBM said typical financial spreadsheet users could encounter an error every 24 days.

"Combine this with the fact that there are millions of Pentium users worldwide, and we quickly come to the conclusion that on a typical day a large number of people are making mistakes in their computations without realizing it," IBM said in a summary of its findings posted on the Internet on Monday.

My assumption is that the difference between the numbers depends on a subjective judgment of how much use is "typical" for an "average" user. Intel surely leaned toward the occasional spreadsheet user, while IBM favored a heavier user.

151 Nonactor winning the Oscar: John Eastman, *Retakes: Behind the Scenes of 500 Classic Movies* (New York: Ballantine, 1989), p. 35.
152 Summing up a client survey: My example is an adaptation of one used by Runyon, p. 70.
155 Heinz 57 varieties: Hay, p. 122.

29 The Sudden Twist

158 Reagan's problem with age: Matthews, p. 157.
159 Rockefeller's speech: Matthews, pp. 161–163.
161 "But Clinton did take on the 1980s . . .": Guy Molyneux, "The Fight to Define the '80's," *Los Angeles Times*, Nov. 22, 1992, Home Edition, sec. M, p. 1.

31 The Dynamics of Buzz

175 "The trend story . . .": Susan Faluti, *Backlash* (New York: Crown, 1991), p. 81.
176 Monkey experiment: see Cialdini, p. 180.
177 Uncertainty and pluralistic ignorance: see Cialdini, pp. 106–113

34 Buzz from Zero

198 "Despite the press coverage . . .": Thomas B. Rosenstiel, "Media Focus on Insiders Misses Big Picture," *Los Angeles Times*, Feb. 12, 1994, Home Edition, sec. A, p. 18.

35 Bad Buzz

200–201 Intel's problem with the Pentium chip: Martha Groves, "Mathematician Finds Intel's Pentium Doesn't Compute," *Los Angeles Times*, Nov. 24, 1994, Home Edition, sec. D, p. 1; Martha Groves, "Pentium Chip Replacement Offered by IBM," *Los Angeles Times*, Dec. 1, 1994, Home Edition, sec. D, p. 1; Martha Groves, "IBM Stops Shipping Pentium PCs," *Los Angeles Times*, Dec. 13, 1994, Home Edition, sec. D, p. 1; Richard O'Reilly, "Does Your PC Have the Pentium Bug?" *Los Angeles Times*, Dec. 13, 1994, Home Edition, sec. D, p. 3; Leslie Helm, "Intel's Handling of the Pentium Defect Chips at Its Image," *Los Angeles Times*, Dec. 13, 1994, Home Edition, sec. D, p. 1; Leslie Helm, "Pentium Chip Flaw Could Leave Intel Liable for Damages," *Los Angeles Times*, Dec. 16, 1994, Home Edition, sec. D, p. 1; David Holley, "Intel's Troubles Greeted in Japan With Quiet Glee," *Los Angeles Times*, Dec. 17, 1994, Home Edition, sec. D, p. 1; Leslie Helm, "Buyers May Be Holding Off on Pentium PCs," *Los Angeles Times*, Dec. 20, 1994, Home Edition, sec. D, p. 1; "Intel Takes $475-Million Earnings Hit," *Los Angeles Times*, Jan. 18, 1995, Home Edition, sec. D, p. 1; Julie Pitta, "Intel Dusts Itself Off, Introduces Chip," *Los Angeles Times*, Feb. 17, 1995, Home Edition, sec. D, p. 3.

BIBLIOGRAPHY

Alessandra, Tony, and Phil Hunsaker. *Communicating at Work*. New York: Fireside, 1993.

Autry, James A. *Love & Profit: The Art of Caring Leadership*. New York: William Morrow, 1991.

Bolton, Robert. *People Skills: How to Assert Yourself, Listen to Others, and Resolve Conflicts*. New York: Touchstone, 1979.

Bridges, Linda, and William F. Rickenbacker. *The Art of Persuasion: A National Review Rhetoric for Writers*. New York: National Review, 1991.

Bryson, Bill. *The Mother Tongue: English and How It Got That Way*. New York: William Morrow, 1990.

Caples, John. *Tested Advertising Methods*. 4th ed. Englewood Cliffs, New Jersey: Prentice-Hall, 1974.

Caro, Robert A. *The Years of Lyndon Johnson: Means of Ascent*. New York: Alfred A. Knopf, 1990.

Caro, Robert A. *The Years of Lyndon Johnson: The Path to Power*. New York: Alfred A. Knopf, 1982.

Cialdini, Robert B. *Influence: Science and Practice*. 3rd ed. New York: HarperCollins College Publishers, 1993.

Damasio, Antonio R. *Descartes' Error: Emotion, Reason, and the Human Brain*. New York: Grosset/Putnam, 1994.

Egri, Lajos. *The Art of Dramatic Writing*. New York: Simon & Schuster, 1946.

Faluti, Susan. *Backlash: The Undeclared War Against American Women*. New York: Crown, 1991.

Fontaine, André, and William A. Glavin Jr. *The Art of Writing Nonfiction*. 2nd ed. Syracuse, New York: Syracuse University Press, 1987.

Gardner, Howard. *Frames of Mind: The Theory of Multiple Intelligences*. New York: BasicBooks, 1983.

Hughes, Richard E., and P. Albert Duhamel. *Rhetoric: Principles and Usage*. Englewood Cliffs, New Jersey: Prentice-Hall, 1962.

Kotler, Philip, and Eduardo L. Roberto. *Social Marketing: Strategies for Changing Public Behavior.* New York: The Free Press, 1989.

Kuhn, Thomas S. *The Structure of Scientific Revolutions.* 2nd ed. Chicago: The University of Chicago Press, 1970.

Leavitt, Harold J. *Managerial Psychology.* 2nd ed. Chicago: The University of Chicago Press, 1969.

Lutz, William. *Doublespeak: From "Revenue Enhancement" to "Terminal Living" How Government, Business, Advertisers, and Others Use Language to Deceive You.* New York: Harper & Row, 1989.

Matthews, Christopher. *Hardball: How Politics Is Played—Told by One Who Knows the Game.* New York: Summit Books, 1988.

McLean, Ruari. *The Thames and Hudson Manual of Typography.* London: Thames and Hudson, 1980.

Ogilvy, David. *Ogilvy on Advertising.* New York: Crown, 1983.

Pinker, Steven. *The Language Instinct: How the Mind Creates Language.* New York: HarperCollins, 1994.

Postman, Neil. *Amusing Ourselves to Death: Public Discourse in the Age of Show Business.* New York: Penguin, 1985.

Pratkanis, Anthony, and Elliot Aronson. *Age of Propaganda: The Everyday Use and Abuse of Persuasion.* New York: W. H. Freeman and Company, 1992.

Rifkin, Jeremy. *Time Wars: The Primary Conflict in Human History.* New York: Touchstone, 1987.

Runyon, Richard P. *How Numbers Lie.* Lexington, Massachusetts: The Lewis Publishing Company, 1981.

Schor, Juliet B. *The Overworked American: The Unexpected Decline of Leisure.* New York: BasicBooks, 1991.

Soden, Garrett. *Looking Good on Paper: How to Create Eye-Catching Reports, Proposals, Memos, and Other Business Documents.* New York: AMACOM, 1995.

Solomon, Jack. *The Signs of Our Time: The Secret Meanings of Everyday Life.* New York: Harper & Row, 1988.

Tannen, Deborah. *You Just Don't Understand: Women and Men in Conversation.* New York: William Morrow, 1990.

Toffler, Alvin. *Powershift: Knowledge, Wealth, and Violence at the Edge of the 21st Century.* New York: Bantam, 1990.

Watkins, Julian Lewis. *The 100 Greatest Advertisements: Who Wrote Them and What They Did.* New York: Dover, 1959.

Weiss, Michael. *The Clustering of America.* New York: Perennial Library, 1988).

White, Jan V. *Editing By Design: Word-and-Picture Communication for Editors and Designers.* New York: R. R. Bowker Co., 1974.

Wright, John S., Daniel S. Warner, Willis L. Winter Jr., and Sherilyn K. Zeigler. *Advertising.* 4th ed. New York: McGraw-Hill, 1977.

INDEX

PETERSON'S/PACESETTER BOOKS

Thinking Books for Thinking Businesspeople

The IdeaFisher
A unique framework for creative thinking
that can be used in everyday working lives.
567-0, 272 pp., $22.95 hc

Frames of Reference
Provocative techniques for improving
communications skills at work.
532-8, 208 pp., $22.95 hc

Getting It Done
An eight-step model for learning how
to use self-discipline.
470-4, 239 pp., $20.95 hc

Techno-Crazed
An entertaining approach to coping
with PCs, modems, and the mysterious
yet wonderful Internet.
570-0, 192 pp., $14.95 pb

21st Century Manager
Outlines a solid management approach that
will work well in both the short and long run.
455-0, 240 pp., $22.95 hc

Peterson's ISBN prefix: 1-56079.

To Order Call
800-338-3282
or Fax
609-243-9150

NEW ON THE INTERNET
Peterson's Career and Education Center
http://www.petersons.com

P Peterson's
Princeton, NJ